IMAGES of America
CUMBERLAND

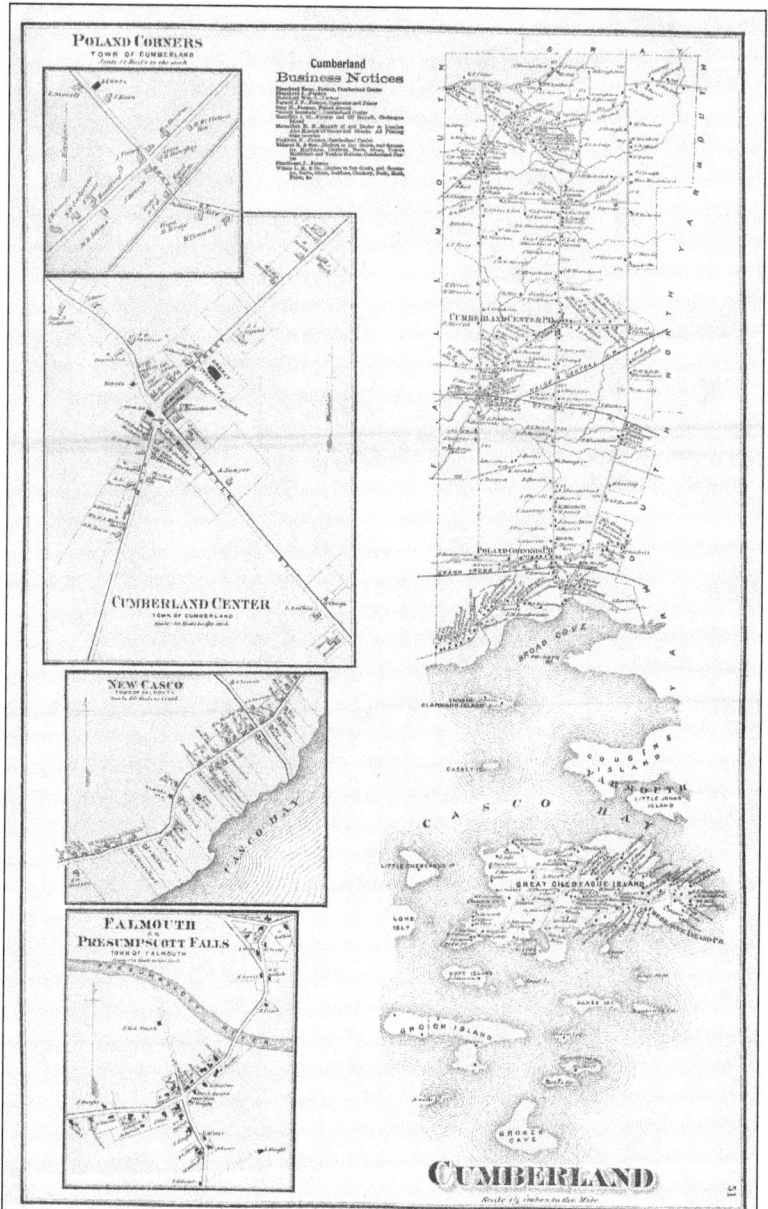

CUMBERLAND, 1871. This is a map of Cumberland from the 1871 Atlas of Cumberland County. (Courtesy of the Cumberland Historical Society and Prince Memorial Library.)

ON THE COVER: RIDEOUT AND SON STORE. After Deacon Humphrey discontinued his Main Street store around 1867, Reuben Rideout, his next-door neighbor, built the R. Rideout and Son Store on the opposite side of the street, next to Silas Rideout's carriage shop. Sometime before 1880, the store was sold to brothers Fenwick and Everett Blanchard, who operated as Blanchard Bros. This photograph was taken during their ownership, before the building burned around 1888. (Courtesy of the Cumberland Historical Society and Prince Memorial Library.)

IMAGES of America
CUMBERLAND

Carolyn Small and Thomas C. Bennett

Copyright © 2021 by Carolyn Small and Thomas C. Bennett
ISBN 9781540246240

Published by Arcadia Publishing
Charleston, South Carolina

Library of Congress Control Number: 2020946303

For all general information, please contact Arcadia Publishing:
Telephone 843-853-2070
Fax 843-853-0044
E-mail sales@arcadiapublishing.com
For customer service and orders:
Toll-Free 1-888-313-2665

Visit us on the Internet at www.arcadiapublishing.com

This book is dedicated to the citizens, past, present, and future, of the Town of Cumberland, Maine.

Contents

Acknowledgments		6
Introduction		7
1.	Church Life	9
2.	Education	21
3.	Business Interests	39
4.	Agriculture	55
5.	Overseers of the Poor	67
6.	Fire Departments	75
7.	Libraries	85
8.	Social Organizations	97
9.	Houses	105
10.	People	117
Bibliography		127

Acknowledgments

Images of America: *Cumberland* would not have been possible without the generosity of the many individuals who shared their photographs and information with Prince Memorial Library and the Cumberland Historical Society. Unless otherwise specified, the images in this book are from the joint collection of the Cumberland Historical Society and Prince Memorial Library. The two institutions are in the process of merging into one location, and going forward, their respective collections will be considered one. The authors would like to thank Jean Bibber, Phil Chase, Mary Dorr Chipman, Joel Fuller, Brian and Lynda Jensen, Nancy Wilson Latham, Kathy Allen Merrill, Becky Quinlan, Phil Stanhope, Dick and Connie Sweetser, Almira Cram Willson, and the countless other individuals who have donated materials to Prince Memorial Library and the Cumberland Historical Society over the decades. Sally Merrill, Steve Moriarty, and Mike Perfetti contributed to the text. Special thanks go out to two highly competent employees of Prince Memorial Library who made the whole thing come together: Yolande Bennett, for her superlative work with the images, and Madeline Grigg, whose original remit was to organize all the textual information from numerous contributors into a semblance of order, but who, in the end, should rightly be considered a co-author due to the quantity and quality of her contributions to the work.

INTRODUCTION

The town of Cumberland, Maine, located on Casco Bay in Cumberland County 11 miles northeast of the city of Portland, was incorporated on March 19, 1821, after a successful secession effort by the residents of the northwestern section of the town of North Yarmouth. In addition to Cumberland, North Yarmouth originally comprised the present-day towns of Yarmouth, North Yarmouth, Pownal, Freeport, Harpswell, and a small part of Brunswick. North Yarmouth was first settled by the English as early as 1635 and was originally known by the native name Westcustogo. Following the conclusion of King Philip's War in 1678, North Yarmouth was incorporated in 1680 as the eighth town in Maine.

Archaeological evidence shows that Cumberland's shoreline was visited by native people going back at least 2,000 years. The more recent history of North Yarmouth included conflict between the area's native populace and the new European arrivals, resulting in a 25-year period beginning in 1690 during which the town was devoid of white settlers. Colonists began returning to the area around 1715, and in 1727, one hundred home lots were created, 64 of which were to be drawn by lot for new settlers. Later, land divisions resulted in the creation of lots of between 100 and 400 acres in size. The area that was to become the town of Cumberland consisted primarily of the 100-acre lots in the southwestern corner of North Yarmouth.

The years following the Revolutionary War witnessed the clearing and settlement of the western section of the town, and, in 1793, the establishment of the Second Church, which stemmed from the 1791 religious revival that saw the conversion of around 150 individuals in North Yarmouth's western section and their desire to worship closer to home. Being some five miles from the First Church, 130 petitioners received from the Massachusetts legislature the right to incorporate the new church, which later was renamed the Congregational Church in Cumberland. The desire of the residents of the western section of North Yarmouth to be closer to their place of worship was mirrored in the 1820 petition filed in the newly minted Maine legislature and signed by 167 male residents seeking the division of the town. The legislature granted an Act of Incorporation the following year, despite the objections of many residents in the eastern part of the town. The new town, which included 22 square miles on the mainland and 18 offshore islands, had a population of 1,386, a figure that increased to 1,713 by 1860.

The town has four distinct areas: Cumberland Center, Cumberland Foreside, West Cumberland, and Chebeague Island. Cumberland Center, the site of the Second Congregational Church of North Yarmouth prior to the secession in 1821, is the center of government and education and is roughly in the geographical middle of the town's boundaries. Cumberland Foreside is the town's coastal mainland area, and although strictly residential for most of the history of the town, was the location of the Poland's Corner neighborhood, which had some businesses, a railroad line, and Spear's shipyard on Broad Cove. The Route 1 corridor, although not directly on the coast, is part of the Foreside. West Cumberland, centered on the Route 100 corridor in the northwest corner of the town, is home to a variety of small businesses. Chebeague Island is the largest island in Casco

Bay and one of only 15 year-round island communities in Maine. In addition to being famous for the stone sloops that carried granite from many of Maine's island quarries, it has traditionally been a fishing, lobstering, and seagoing community. Chebeague was granted independence from the Town of Cumberland by the Maine legislature and became a town on July 1, 2007.

Mainland Cumberland's economy has traditionally included farming and shipbuilding, and the town was home to dozens of saw, grist, and stave mills. Business listings for Cumberland in the *Maine Register* over the years attest to the rural nature of the town, and commerce was unmistakably of an extractive nature or supportive of agriculture.

The 1920 US Census numbered the town's residents at 1,150; the previous decade had seen an 18 percent decrease in Cumberland's population. The town had reached its 20th-century population nadir, leaving the populace at virtually the same number as at the community's founding nearly a century prior. By 1930, when the country had just entered the Great Depression and the town's population was within eight residents of the number it had on its founding more than a century before, Cumberland's economy reflected its inhabitants' needs. Subsistence farming and diversified livestock production helped sustain the residents, and the town's proximity to Portland allowed the inhabitants to work in the city while living in a rural setting. As it had during the initial population increase between 1821 and 1860, Cumberland welcomed new residents. The newcomers did little to alter the town, joining the churches that were in existence rather than starting their own, changing the community's framework by their numbers and birth rates and not their bloodlines and institutions. The town's farmers, like all farmers in Maine, had responded before to necessity and would continue to do so, just as those who previously rode the electric cars into Portland or Lewiston or Yarmouth would now use the ubiquitous automobile for their transportation needs.

The population more than doubled by 1960, and the rapid growth resulted in the creation of the Cumberland Planning Board in 1955 and the board's membership in the Greater Portland Regional Planning Commission. One of the new board's first significant actions was the issuance of the 1958 Comprehensive Plan, which described the community as a "bedroom town" whose residents were as likely to work in Portland as in Cumberland. By 2010, the town's population was 7,211.

Welcoming newcomers, adapting in the face of want, and taking care of one's own were the hallmarks of community evident in small towns throughout the country. Cumberland, borne of North Yarmouth and since surpassing its mother town in terms of population and economic activity, recovered from its own loss of populace and shift in agricultural fortunes, welcoming new residents to what would become another of Portland's bedroom communities, allowing its inhabitants to benefit from the nearness of Maine's largest city while residing in a pastoral location.

One
CHURCH LIFE

The shores of Aucocisco Bay must have appeared forbidding to the earliest European explorers and settlers. The area known as Westcustogo eventually became ancient North Yarmouth, which included today's Cumberland. Churches were established to provide spiritual support to the settlers and played a key role in defining the separate communities that formed from the original territory. In 1730, the Church under the Ledge was organized off Route 88 in present-day Yarmouth. As settlement gradually spread inland, travel to the original church became increasingly difficult. In 1793, residents of Cumberland Center and the Walnut Hill area petitioned Massachusetts to form a new church, and permission was granted. The new church, then called the Second Church in North Yarmouth, built its meetinghouse at the corner of Blanchard Road and Main Street. After Cumberland seceded from North Yarmouth in 1821, the Second Church became the Congregational Church in Cumberland, as it is still known today. In 1831, to make room for a new county road, the original building was demolished and rebuilt at its current location on Main Street, using timbers from the first meetinghouse. Although the Congregational church was a central fixture in Cumberland at the time, other churches grew out of the divergent beliefs and needs of the community. In 1789, a Methodist meetinghouse was built where Falmouth and Cumberland adjoin on Foreside Road. In 1944, the Methodists withdrew, and the sanctuary became the Foreside Community Church, which in 1968 affiliated with the United Church of Christ. Two other Methodist churches were established in town. In the early 1800s, the Methodist Episcopal Church was founded in West Cumberland and joined by the Universalists. Under the name Universalist Society, the church held services until 1958. The First Methodist Episcopal Church was reestablished in 1963, and a parish hall was built on the corner of Methodist and Blackstrap Roads. The Tuttle Road United Methodist Church was built at its current location in 1882.

OLD MEETING HOUSE UNDER THE LEDGE, YARMOUTH, MAINE

CHURCH UNDER THE LEDGE. This is a sketch of the first church established in North Yarmouth. Known as the Church under the Ledge, the building was constructed in 1730 in present-day Yarmouth in the area of Route 88 and Prince's Point Road. For many years, it was the only church in the area and served growing but widely separated settled portions of ancient North Yarmouth. Although the church no longer exists, its doorstep still serves as a front step for one of the homes in the area, and a number of other churches in the region eventually formed from it. Settlement moved inland and westward in the years following the Revolutionary War, and a religious revival in 1791 spurred a movement to establish a new church. Permission was obtained from Massachusetts in 1793 to form a new church to serve the needs of the current Cumberland Center and Walnut Hill areas.

CONGREGATIONAL CHURCH IN CUMBERLAND, C. 1905. The new church was originally known as the Second Church in North Yarmouth, and in 1794, a small square structure was built at the corner of Blanchard Road and Main Street. After Cumberland became independent from North Yarmouth in 1821, the church changed its name to the Congregational Church in Cumberland, by which it is still known. The original building was constructed too close to the road and was demolished, and a new sanctuary was constructed in 1831 adjacent to the original site. At right is a front view of the church in its current location. The photograph below, taken around 1905, shows the Congregational Church in Cumberland and the extensive stables that served the needs of the parishioners. Many members traveled by horseback or wagon to attend services, as the church served a broad geographical region.

CONGREGATIONAL CHURCH IN CUMBERLAND. In 1916, the sanctuary was raised to create a vestry below, and the new front-entry stairs can clearly be seen in this panoramic photograph. The stables are on the left; this area is now a parking lot. To the immediate right of the church is the former Red Men's Hall, which is the current home of Sevee & Maher Engineers. At far right, a portion of the 1853 District Three brick schoolhouse, which would later serve as the Cumberland

Town Hall, can be seen. Since 1989, the former schoolhouse has been home to the Cumberland Historical Society. In May 2020, the building was moved a short distance to the grounds of the Prince Memorial Library, where it will be renovated for continued service as headquarters to the Historical Society.

CONGREGATIONAL CHURCH PARSONAGE. The 306 Main Street brick parsonage seen here was added during the time of Rev. Joseph Blake, pastor from 1841 to 1859. The bricks were made in the old kiln behind where Prince Memorial Library now stands. Blake planted elm trees all around the parsonage and church, although many were later affected by Dutch elm disease. In the following years, the church lost members in the Civil War and to westward emigration.

CONGREGATIONAL CEMETERY. This photograph was taken from the steeple looking north along Main Street. The Congregational Cemetery is in the foreground, across the intersection with Tuttle Road. Beyond the cemetery, Greely Institute, built in 1868, rises as the largest structure in Cumberland Center.

CONGREGATIONAL CHURCH IN CUMBERLAND, 1943. In 1878, Rev. T.S. Perry noted that the Congregational church was notable for the large number of attendees from certain families: "Of all the members of this church, not less than seventy-five have borne the name of Blanchard; forty-six the name of Prince; forty-eight the name of Sweetser; thirty that of Merrill, and many other names often recur in the lists of this church."

THE CONGREGATIONAL CHURCH'S 150TH ANNIVERSARY. In 1943, the church celebrated the 150th anniversary of its founding. During the morning service, most of the congregation dressed as their ancestors to recognize the church's long history. A happy group of parishioners gathered on the front steps to mark the occasion. Among those present were members of the Barter, Blanchard, Burnell, Chase, Doane, Fickett, Porter, Wyman, and Warren families.

BLANCHARD FAMILY AT THE 150TH ANNIVERSARY. Proud and happy, Arthur and Joanne Blanchard stand with three of their four daughters on the front lawn of the church at the 1943 sesquicentennial. At the time, the Blanchards resided in the former Prince Tavern at the corner of Main Street and Tuttle Road, now the home of the Cumberland Food Company.

CONGREGATIONAL CHURCH PARISH HALL. To accommodate the needs of a growing congregation, the parish hall was built in 1964 and dedicated that year. The upper floor contained a large meeting room, a kitchen, and pastoral offices. The lower floor housed Sunday school classrooms. In 1989, a connector was built linking the sanctuary with the Parish Hall.

FORESIDE METHODIST EPISCOPAL CHURCH. During the same time the Second Church was forming, the First Methodist Church had its beginnings on the Falmouth-Cumberland town line on Foreside Road. Services were held in a log structure beginning in 1789, and after the first and second meetinghouses were burned, the present church was built in 1811. The Foreside Methodist Episcopal Church is shown here in 1910. Originally, parishioners from the two towns sat on separate sides, and sermons were delivered from both sides of the pulpit to the two halves of the congregation. Following the withdrawal of the Methodists in 1944, the church took on the name of the Foreside Community Church. In 1968, the church joined with the United Church of Christ. Over the years, the original sanctuary was expanded, a cellar was built in 1920, and a fellowship hall was added in 1953. In 1981, a Sunday school addition was built, followed by new church offices in 1998.

FIRST METHODIST EPISCOPAL CHURCH. In time, two other Methodist churches were established in town. The First Methodist Episcopal Church formed in West Cumberland in 1800 and was joined by the Universalists in erecting a meetinghouse in 1813. By 1825, the congregation was led by Rev. James Jacques and had 15 members, including John Marston and his wife, Sarah, and members from the Jordan, Brackett, and Winslow families. The meetinghouse was rebuilt and dedicated in 1848, and after a long closure was reactivated in 1963. Annie C. Copp donated a parcel of land on the corner of Blackstrap and Methodist Roads, and a meetinghouse was constructed. A parish hall was built near the church and dedicated by Bishop Matthews in 1969. By the 1970s, there were nearly 40 regular members on the rolls of the church.

WEST CUMBERLAND UNITED METHODIST CHURCH. This photograph shows the Methodist Episcopal Church, now known as the West Cumberland United Methodist Church, as it appeared in 1973. A 1997 addition to the hall created space for the pastor's office, together with a necessary storage room. Another church in the area, the Universalist Society, met for a time in the 1800s and early 1900s. In 1847, the Universalist Society received land from Ephraim Morrison on Morrison Hill in West Cumberland for its own church along present-day Route 100. In June 1869, Morrison deeded another 10 rods in the back for a burying ground. Over time, however, the church was neglected, and the cemetery was in sad condition. In the 1920s, women who had attended the church in their youth organized a movement to care for both the yard and the church, which reopened in the summers with services conducted by Harry Townsend from the Westbrook Universalist Church. The land was sold to the Pentecostal Society of the Apostolic Challenge in 1958.

TUTTLE ROAD UNITED METHODIST CHURCH. The Tuttle Road United Methodist Church, above the intersection of Middle Road, was founded and built in 1882. Before the church was built, the church's Falmouth-Cumberland community was organized by circuit riders and preachers from Portland. In 1924, Alfred W. Doughty donated a building for social functions. The church itself was enlarged in 1947 and again in 1967. A larger sanctuary was built in 1992–1993 to accommodate the growing congregation, and the smaller, older building became a space for Sunday school. In 1999, a narthex connecting the old and new buildings was constructed, and the old church was renovated to create a pastor's office, Sunday school room, and a small chapel. Many of the original features of the old building were preserved for possible future conversion into a chapel.

Two

Education

Cumberland has been educating young people since 1790, the year the Misses Martins' School for Young Ladies was founded by the daughters of English immigrants William and Elizabeth Martin. In 1821, just after Maine became a state, local records indicate the selectmen of the town appropriated $550 ($12,500 today) for the education of students ages five to twenty-five. One-room schools were scattered throughout the town, each with its own teacher responsible for all students. Students had the responsibility of providing their own books. Each district within the town was supervised by an agent to monitor and, if necessary, replace unsatisfactory teachers. As a result, education and opportunity at these schoolhouses varied drastically from schoolhouse to schoolhouse and hinged on the quality of the teacher, the students' home lives, and the resources of the school itself, which could be limited by the student population, funding, and (in the case of island schools) access to mainland resources. At the age of 12, students graduated to Greely Institute, which was founded in 1868 from money and land donated by husband and wife Eliphalet and Sarah Loring Greely. Early in the institute's history, and with strong municipal financial support, the student population stood at 200 by 1872. Unfortunately, the selectmen's interest in funding the school soon declined, and over time, attendance dropped to 35. In 1913, the state incorporated the institute, and the town appropriated $1,000 to operate it. In 1950, Cumberland Elementary School was built, effectively ending the era of schoolhouse education. In 1966, Cumberland and North Yarmouth joined together to form Maine School Administrative District 51 (MSAD 51), and Greely Institute was renamed Greely High School. The following year, the new Mabel I. Wilson School welcomed elementary students, and in 2004, Greely Middle School opened to students.

MISSES MARTINS' SCHOOL FOR YOUNG LADIES. William Martin, a London businessman, purchased this house from Jeremiah Powell in 1788. In 1790, his English-educated daughter Penelope transformed the home into a private school for girls. With her sisters Eliza and Catherine, Penelope ran the Misses Martins' School for Young Ladies until 1804, when the family relocated to Portland. The Martins' school was one of the first in Maine to offer a thorough curriculum and higher education to women. Other private schools were held in old homes, including the schools at Top Knot farm on Middle Road, which was managed by William Buxton and his wife, Maria. At the first Cumberland town meeting in 1821, a total of $550 was set aside to support the town schools. Each schoolhouse was assigned one teacher, who was expected to teach a class of students that varied widely in both age and educational needs.

DISTRICT TWO TUTTLE ROAD SCHOOL. The Tuttle Road school was a typical one-room schoolhouse with separate entries for boys and girls. Originally on Harris Road, the building was moved by oxen in 1854 to its current location, diagonally across from the Tuttle Road Methodist Church. In a 1986 interview, Robert Cram recalled, "It was one room, nine grades, one teacher, two stoves on each end of the building, wood stoves, and we went across the street to get a pail of water and that was about the luxury we had." According to school reports from 1865 through 1906, the schoolhouse on Tuttle Road was often plagued with issues that hindered academic progress. Observers noted that the teachers for the term would likely excel at any other school and that District Two required a very specific type of teacher.

TUTTLE ROAD SCHOOL, CLARA ANDERSON'S CLASS. The 1901 school report suggests that the academic and disciplinary problems stemmed from home, saying, "Home influence affects schools the most of any known thing. It is too much to expect of a teacher that she shall smooth away family feuds of years standing. The next teacher in No. 2 should be a disciplinarian of tried experience and, if necessary, she should be aided in her efforts to secure order. An unfortunate condition of affairs holds here." From left to right, this Tuttle Road school class includes (first row) Desmond O'Conor, Marshall Cram, Harry Morrell, Clifton O'Conor, and Elton Cram; (second row) unidentified, Katharin Doughty, Della Cram, Berta Brown, Anna Larsen, Elsie Bryden, Vena Mahar, Gertrude Brown, and Marie Larsen; (third row) Lloyd Bryden, Hannah Chapman, Andus Larsen, Verona Bryden, John Larsen, Elna Larsen, Robert Cram, teacher Clara Anderson, and Laura Mahar.

TUTTLE ROAD SCHOOL, MRS. STAPLES'S CLASS. Observers also noted that the Tuttle Road pupils' knowledge of subjects like mental arithmetic, geography, and history were next to none. Despite these challenges, however, the Tuttle Road school was, under the right supervision, sometimes considered one of the best in town. After it closed in 1950, it became a private dwelling. A Tuttle Road class poses here. From left to right are (first row), Greely Sturdivant, Desmond O'Conor, Wallace Brown, Clifton O'Conor, Marshall Cram, John Larsen, Harry Morrell, Alfred Staples, and Eugene Staples; (second row) Elton Cram, Marie Larsen, Anna Larsen, unidentified, Bertha Brown, Vena Mahar, Elsie Bryden, Laura Mahar, Verona Bryden, and Lloyd Bryden; (third row) Elna Larsen, Elton Peterson, Alice Sturdivant, Andus Larsen, unidentified, Randall Doughty, Hannah Chapman, Robert Cram, and teacher Mrs. Staples.

DISTRICT THREE CUMBERLAND CENTER SCHOOL. The District Three schoolhouse was built in 1853 to replace the original wooden schoolhouse across the road, which burned. Later distinguished as Cumberland Center Primary, it housed one of the largest classes in the area. Rita McCloskey recalls the schoolhouse when E.K. Sweetser taught in the 1880s, "with its double seats and desks, the two stoves for warmth in winter, the teacher's ready bell, and that pail of water with the old familiar dipper shared by all." After the District Three school was closed in 1950, the building became the new town office from 1951 to 1975. Following a fire in 1955, the building was renovated to include an addition with a fireproof vault, two flush toilets, and a furnace room. Later, it housed the police department and, most recently, the Cumberland Historical Society.

E.K. Sweetser School. Although he only taught for three years at the District Three school before returning in 1891, Ezra K. Sweetser's commitment to education left an impression on the Cumberland community. The school district agent who observed his class in 1881 reported that, under his management, the Tuttle Road school "was one of the best in town" and that Sweetser was "just the teacher needed" for the class. Sweetser provided land for a new public grammar school, which was named E.K. Sweetser School and opened in 1914. The school served grades seven and eight until 1954. Today, the building houses the administrative offices for MSAD 51.

WEST CUMBERLAND SHAWTOWN SCHOOL AND GREELY ROAD SCHOOL. Throughout the 1800s, the District Four Shawtown School (above) was often credited with having some of the brightest students in Cumberland and enjoyed a relatively high attendance rate. For a time, the school received students from District Twelve on Blackstrap Road before they were sent to Falmouth schools. After Cumberland's one-room schools were closed in 1950, the Shawtown school was converted into the current J. Brothers Variety store on Route 100. In this photograph are, from left to right, Huldah Peterson, Tillie Leighton, Lydia Legrow, Linwood Morrill, three unidentified, teacher Lizzie Copp, Clement Field, Mads Petersen, Noland ?, and Clifton Copp. Below is the District Six Greely Road School, which was under the supervision of the Yarmouth School District for several years, despite officially falling under Cumberland's jurisdiction.

DISTRICT SEVEN WINN ROAD SCHOOL. The Winn Road school, at the intersection of Winn, Range, and Cross Roads, was built in 1848. An excerpt from *Maine: An Encyclopedia* describes the school as "one of only two known surviving one-room, brick, Greek Revival schoolhouses in Maine, the other, also in Cumberland, has been substantially altered. . . . Little remains of its original interior, but a sloping floor, allowing a teacher to keep an eye on students, remained in 1983." The building was used briefly as a salt shed after the school closed. It was listed in the National Register of Historic Places in 1984. Today, it is privately owned. Below, Francis Small (left) and Al Taylor stand in front of the former schoolhouse during its days as a salt shed.

Greely Institute, c. 1870. In 1858, Eliphalet Greely willed $27,500 to the town of Cumberland for the establishment of what would become Greely Institute and, much later, Greely High School. Greely amassed a significant fortune over his life, having served as the president of Casco National Bank for 33 years and Portland's mayor for five years. Although he had no children of his own, Greely wanted the children of his hometown, from ages 12 to 21, to have free access to education. His widow, Elizabeth Loring Greely, gave four acres of barren pasture for the site of the school, and Greely Institute opened on September 28, 1868. The photograph above shows Greely Institute around 1870, only a few years after its opening. Initially, the building included a study hall, classroom, combined principal's office and library, and a large room for assemblies on the second floor. In June 1880, Greely held its first graduation for six students: Roland Blanchard, Addie Dunn, Annie Leighton, Edward B. Osgood, Lena Pinkham, and Edward Warren.

GREELY INSTITUTE, C. 1955 (ABOVE) AND 1961 (BELOW). For several years, the school operated on $250 a year with only two teachers and the occasional student assistant while attendance hovered around 35 or 40. By the 1870s, attendance had once again risen to nearly 200 students, including some pupils from other towns. In 1913, Greely Institute was incorporated, and in 1914, the town appropriated $1,000 for improvements, allowing the school to become a class-A high school, which allowed graduates to enter college without taking external examinations. Classes in agriculture and home economics became part of the regular curriculum, and a house at 310 Main Street was remodeled to include a dormitory, home economics classroom, and laboratory.

GREELY INSTITUTE CLASS OF 1933. Greely faculty and the class of 1933 pose in front of Greely Institute. In his report for that year, Greely principal Otto W. Davis wrote, "I feel we have a well-rounded program for a school of this size. By the inclusion of the courses in Sociology, Economics, and Business Training, the latitude for choice of subjects has been made broader for those pupils

not planning to continue their schooling beyond the Institute. At the same time, the college preparatory students have not been penalized as it is yet possible to study four years of Latin and two years of French."

GREELY INSTITUTE, 1923. Students and staff of the Greely Institute are arranged for a photograph on the school grounds in 1923. In the center of the first row, as well as in the top-right inset, are three members of Greely Institute staff (from left to right): teacher M.E. Norell, principal Howard Winslow, and an unidentified teacher.

GYGER GYMNASIUM. The new school gymnasium, built under the auspices of the federal Public Works Administration, was named in honor of John T. Gyger, superintendent between 1928 and 1939, who died one week before the building's dedication on June 9, 1939. The basement housed agriculture and shop classes, as well as modern toilets, locker rooms, and showers for athletic activities. Beginning in 1947, the gymnasium hosted the annual town meeting.

UNION HALL. In 1914, the alumni association bought the Union Hall building (previously an exhibition hall for the fair, a vestry for the Congregational church, and the Red Men's meeting space) to use as a gymnasium for Greely Institute. In 1916, the kitchen was remodeled for the home economics cooking laboratory, and Lucille Clark started the first hot lunch program for schoolchildren in Cumberland. When Gyger Gymnasium was completed in 1939, the newly freed space at Union Hall was repurposed for a farmer's workshop arranged by William Farwell, the agriculture teacher. In 1948, the building was refitted for a two-room junior high school. The foundation supports were replaced, the floor strengthened, the walls braced, and the ceiling lowered. Partitions and closets were added, as well as a new heating system and toilets. After 1961 it became the school cafeteria, and later was used as overflow classrooms and as the office of the superintendent of schools.

CUMBERLAND ELEMENTARY SCHOOL. The Drowne Farm was a 100-acre plot that remained as originally laid out by the first surveyors of Cumberland, which was willed to the town in 1907 by Elizabeth Sturdivant Drowne for educational purposes. Under the purview of Supt. William H. Soule, in 1950, a consolidated elementary school opened on the Drowne Farm for grades kindergarten through sixth, and a four-room school opened on Chebeague Island to replace the former system of one-room schoolhouses. The Cumberland Elementary School contained nine classrooms, a hot lunch kitchen, a teacher's room, an office, and an oil-fired steam heater in the basement. Despite this accomplishment, the 1960s saw an increased demand for school spaces as kindergarten and elementary classes grew in size. The building served as Cumberland Town Hall for a period and has since been turned into senior housing.

NEW GREELY HIGH SCHOOL, 1961. In the 1950s, Cumberland schools became crowded as the school district struggled to keep pace with the town's growing population. Additional classes were housed in the old Union Hall and the Red Men's Hall. Determining that it was only a matter of time before Greely Institute was inadequate for its students, Cumberland school and survey committees went ahead with a three-part plan for expansion, which included adding the new high school (pictured), Cumberland Elementary School, a science wing, and a new gymnasium, with classes shuffled from building to building as new spaces opened up. Renovation began in 1961 with the first of several anticipated renovations, and 12 new classrooms were added to the Greely complex. By 1965, Greely High School boasted 294 students and a town budget of $151,000.

MABEL I. WILSON SCHOOL GROUND BREAKING. In 1957, through subsidies and other financial measures, the Sinclair Act encouraged small towns in Maine to organize into districts with a minimum high school enrollment of 300 students. In February 1966, Cumberland and North Yarmouth merged school districts, officially forming Maine School Administrative District 51, and Greely Institute was renamed Greely High School. The school committee made plans for further additions, including a new gymnasium, swimming pool, auditorium, music room, and locker rooms. As part of the transition from Cumberland's independent school district to MSAD 51, the committee also made plans for a 16-room elementary school with a multipurpose room, kitchen facilities, and an administrative section, with room for expansion. In September 1966, the board of directors voted to name the school for Mabel I. Wilson to honor her commitment to and involvement in the local school system. The school was ready for occupancy in September 1967. In this photograph, Wilson helps break ground for the new school's construction.

Three
BUSINESS INTERESTS

The earliest businesses arose from the community's immediate needs: farms, taverns, blacksmiths, general stores, shipyards, sawmills, and other small, local commercial establishments. The Prince Tavern in Cumberland Center and the Leighton Tavern in West Cumberland served the needs of travelers and locals alike. One of the first well-known general stores in this area belonged to Charles Poland, which sold staples like molasses, butter, flour, tea, fish, pork, coffee, salt, and other supplies. When Poland's shop closed, other general stores opened in Cumberland and often doubled as post offices and meeting places. The Spear shipyard at Town Landing was responsible for building over 50 ships, including the famed clipper *Grapeshot*. Agricultural pursuits, which will be discussed in more detail in the next chapter, included fruit and dairy farming, raising beef cattle, trout fishing, and carnation cultivation. As the railroad and industrialization reached Maine, the business model changed in scale and scope. Steam rail lines made transportation easier, making distant markets more accessible and specialization in one product more profitable, and Cumberland Junction became a center of activity in the town. Processing and packing plants set up shop nearby, including Merrill Brothers (established in 1881) and the Herricks. Both facilities mainly canned corn, but also other vegetables, fruits, and meat. By the early 1900s, the junction saw at least 40 trains a day carrying goods to and from Cumberland. Another leading business at the time included poultry farmers like Gilbert Strout, Harvey Blanchard, and Willis and Walter Thurston. Their workers, mostly women, processed and packed poultry for shipment to Boston, New York, and elsewhere. Soon after, the electric trolley system made day trips more possible, and fashionable attractions like teahouses, hotels, and the Gray Animal Zoo had their heyday in the early 1900s, marking the advent of the tourism industry in Cumberland.

THE PRINCE TAVERN AND THE LEIGHTON TAVERN. Later the Blanchard Broadmoor Farm, the Prince Tavern (above) was built in the mid-1700s on land purchased from Jeremiah Powell by yeoman James Prince. The old stagecoach road from Falmouth (now Portland) to Bakertown (now Lewiston) ran through the arch of the tavern, where horses could be changed from the tavern's 15-stall stable and travelers' luggage carried into the tavern. Today, the Prince Tavern is the Cumberland Food Company. The Leighton Tavern (below), built around 1800, is the oldest and most familiar tavern in Cumberland and was on the Portland-Lewiston stagecoach road. The builder and original proprietor, Andrew Leighton, who had seven sons and a single daughter named Mercy, died in 1830, but the building remained in the Leighton family for over a century. In 1970, it was relocated to Schooner Rocks as a private residence.

POLAND'S CORNER. Poland's Corner was named for Charles Poland (1795–1867), who opened a store on the corner of Middle and Tuttle Roads in 1840. He lived there with his wife, Eunice Harris, and their nine children. They converted the basement kitchen of the home into a store, which quickly became an area staple. In 1871, Hollis Doughty opened another store at Poland's Corner, which he later sold to John E. Dunn and his father, John N. Dunn. In 1876, J.E. Dunn built a new store across the road from the old one and owned the business for about 20 years. Dunn sold the store to E.H. Trickey, who in turn sold to his former employees Frank H. Jones and Alfred W. Doughty. Jones and Doughty partnered until 1900, when Doughty became the sole proprietor until 1923. Poland's original store was demolished in the 1920s by J.N. Dunn.

TRUE BLACKSMITH SHOP AND SILAS RIDEOUT'S WORKSHOP. Mary Sweetser recalls Samuel True's blacksmith shop in the 1850s in *History of the Town of Cumberland*: "A blacksmith's shop stood very near the well and a big elm tree on what is now the property of Fred Adams. The old familiar sign, Samuel True, Blacksmith with a prancing black horse painted at one end and a horseshoe at the other was fastened near the edge of the roof over the doors. . . . Colonel True and his son Edward carried on the business for many years." In addition to blacksmithing, True served as the town's postmaster for 26 years. Below, Silas Rideout builds furniture in his carpentry workshop in 1898. Rideout had a carriage business in a shop beside his home. Surviving receipts from the 1850s and 1860s show Rideout also furnished coffins in Cumberland.

EDWARD WILSON STORE AND ADAMS BLACKSMITH SHOP. Around 1828, Capt. Edward Wilson moved his business from Tuttle Road to a new location just south of the Congregational church. Rooms over the store allowed his family to live conveniently nearby. Around 1832, Wilson sold to Isaac Merrill, who ran the store for 20 years. Nathaniel Humphrey bought the store around 1857 and sold it to Frank Hall at the beginning of his medical career. Tragically, he died only five years later, and his brother Dr. Milton Hall took over the practice. Later, Oren Thomes bought the place, and eventually Fred Adams, who built his blacksmith shop beside it, took it over. The blacksmith shop, located near the church, was where the majority of the town had their horses shod. Since shoeing horses took time, chairs were provided for customers to sit and converse.

N.B. Wilson Store. Brothers William and Lorenzo Wilson established their store in 1854. The first floor served as the general store and housed the West Cumberland Post Office, while the second floor was used for teaching, dancing, and community gatherings. Eventually, Lorenzo left for the sawmill business, and in 1873, a cousin, Nathaniel Baker Wilson, acquired the property. His son Alvah inherited the store. Eva Pride bought the property after Alvah died in 1912.

Allen Farm Stand. A more recent local business in West Cumberland is Allen's Farm Stand, later called Allen Farm Country Store, on Gray Road. In 1957, Robert and Kathleen Copp Allen (pictured) opened a grocery store and farm stand on their 35-acre plot, where they sold farm produce and novelties. Their four children were also involved in running the business. (Courtesy of Kathy Allen Merrill.)

JAMES L. DUNN STORE. The J.L. Dunn store was built on the site of the former Blanchard Brothers store. In January 1878, *The Cumberland Globe* ran a notice that read, "The brothers F.S. and E.L. Blanchard have bought the store of York & Doughty, and will run a general store under the firm name Blanchard Bros. With commendable spirit, they propose to ship their own corn direct from the West, and supply farmers at cheaper rates than heretofore. Will grind their own corn as soon as they make arrangements for steam power." The Blanchard Brothers building burned around 1888, and the J.L. Dunn General Store operated from 1890 until 1923. The store was later managed by other merchants, including T.R. Jordan, Paul Merrill, and Howard Call. The building had apartments on the second floor. By 1960, the store had closed and the building was converted to all apartments. (Courtesy of Mary Dorr Chipman.)

CUMBERLAND DEPOT. This photograph shows Cumberland Depot along the Atlantic & St. Lawrence Railroad, one of two steam rail lines through Cumberland, which opened in 1848 and later became the Grand Trunk Railway. The other station, Cumberland Junction along the Maine Central Railroad, opened in 1871 and became an industrial hub, shipping canned goods, fresh flowers, cured meats, poultry, eggs, and other Cumberland goods to Boston and beyond. In 1900, Cumberland Junction was the center of economic activity within the town. The many trains that stopped there each day not only took the local product to market, but also delivered to the town's residents their dry goods, furniture, and other items ordered from the stores in Portland, the wharves of Bath, and mail-order businesses in other parts of the country. Half of the 40 trains passing through Cumberland Junction during the early 1900s were passenger trains.

EDWARD TRICKEY STORE AND POST OFFICE. Cumberland Depot, built in Poland's Corner on Tuttle Road, was also the home of the post office when John N. Dunn, station agent for the Grand Trunk Railway, became postmaster in 1870. In 1895, the post office moved to this store at the corner of Middle and Tuttle Roads when Edward H. Trickey was named postmaster, and it remained there until 1918. During the height of train travel, a train went to and from Montreal every day, carrying grain, flour, and other supplies. The station was destroyed by a fire and closed in 1923; it was used for a time as a way station. Following World War II, as the need for gasoline rationing disappeared and automobiles became more accessible, Maine Central Railroad and other steam rails struggled to keep passengers. The final scheduled passenger train passed through Cumberland in September 1960.

STANLEY CATTLE AUCTION. This panoramic photograph was taken by Cumberland native Floyd Norton from atop a railroad car. The Cumberland Junction station is on the right. The many people attending the auction can be seen clustered around the house porch at center. While

many parked their automobiles between the house and the train station, others who traveled by horse-drawn vehicle tied their horses to various fences on the left near the larger barn. Many of the horses, still in their traces, are covered with blankets to protect them from the weather.

E.B. Osgood Delivery Wagons. Edward B. "Deacon" Osgood started butchering pigs around 1890 and sold meat from a small store next to his butcher shop. He smoked ham and bacon on the premises and made sausages following his own secret recipe. A New Hampshire company aged country cheese specifically for his business. In addition to his butcher shop, Osgood ran a packing plant that, by 1940, averaged 5,914 pounds of lard, 3,245 pounds of sausage, and 14 tons of ham and bacon per year. Each spring, Osgood and his crew worked a 20-acre patch devoted to market gardening. Osgood's grandson Fred took over the business after his death in 1944. (Both, courtesy of Joel Fuller.)

MOUNTFORTS MILL. Mainland Cumberland was home to dozens of saw, grist, carding, and stave mills over the years. John Powell built a sawmill and gristmill on Felt's Brook above Broad Cove around 1730. Mill Brook in West Cumberland was home to at least six mills, including Mountforts Mill (pictured). Five mills were on Mill Road in 1871, with others on Gray Road and the brook between Blanchard and Range Roads.

SKILLINS ROAD DAM AND MILL. Many streams and rivers in Maine provided ripe power sources for water-powered mills. The need for building materials increased rapidly with New England's population, and eventually there were mills on most rivers and streams. Most sawmills were small, with a single saw, and integral to the local economy. Cumberland was no exception. This mill on Skillins Road later became a private residence. (Courtesy of Phil Chase.)

PORTLAND-LEWISTON INTERURBAN RAILROAD CAR. On November 31, 1894, it was announced that the Portland & Yarmouth Electric Railway would pass through Cumberland, providing a more convenient mode of transportation than the steam railway. Regular service began in August 1898, following the route from Monument Square in Portland to Yarmouth along what would later become Route 88. In 1914, the Portland-Lewiston Interurban Railroad began service through West Cumberland. With the ability to travel longer distances with ease at an affordable fare, hotels, tearooms, and other attractions soon became common in the area. Portland & Yarmouth Electric built the Underwood Springs pleasure resort, complete with casino and shore dinners, to draw more traffic through the area. West Cumberland's farmers relied on the interurban to ship their milk and farm produce to Portland and the Lewiston-Auburn area. As the automobile usurped both steam and electric rail lines in terms of convenience, ridership on the trolley lines declined, and both the Portland & Yarmouth Electric Railway and the Portland-Lewiston Interurban Railroad ended service on June 28, 1933.

THE WILDWOOD INN. In 1909, Sumner Sturdivant sold the Wildwood property on Foreside Road to Herman P. Rausch and Concord Realty, who developed a community of summer cottages on the land along with an inn, restaurant, and teahouse. Customers entered the inn and paid for their dinner, passed through the Japanese Room, and had their meals on the porch, which accommodated eight spacious oak tables, each large enough to seat 10 people. The inn's famous "shore dinners" added to the appeal of Wildwood's beachside properties and drew both locals and out-of-state tourists to the area. Most visitors arrived on the trolley line that ran from Portland to Yarmouth along Foreside Road. The next few decades transformed Wildwood. With the advent of automobiles, the trolley line became less popular, and was abandoned by 1933. During World War II, Wildwood experienced a period of neglect, during which conditions in the park deteriorated. By 1959, however, the *Press Herald* described Wildwood as a year-round residential area occupied by middle-income couples with children. (Courtesy of Becky Quinlan.)

PRIDE'S FOREST TEA ROOM AND GRAY ROAD AMUSEMENT PARK AND ZOO. Pride's Forest Tea Room on Route 100 and Blackstrap Road was one of the many teahouses that cropped up in Maine in the 1910s. In the photograph above, a sign advertises chicken dinners, chicken pies, crab meat sandwiches, hot waffles, salads, coffee, and donuts among the tea room's offerings. The Gray Road Amusement Park and Zoo (below) was another of the attractions that existed when the Portland-Lewiston Interurban Railroad ran through town. The zoo boasted alligators and exotic birds. As seen on the sign, fried clams and other food was also sold there. Nearby, on the northwest corner of Blackstrap and Gray Roads, Spinney's Gray Road Inn was a popular dance hall that attracted young and old alike from around the Greater Portland area. The building was demolished in the 1970s.

Four

AGRICULTURE

Cumberland's farmers grew a variety of products, most notably potatoes, hay, and corn. At least two canneries, Merrill Brothers and Herricks, supported agriculture over the years and provided seasonal employment for many of the town's young people. Both facilities canned primarily corn as well as other vegetables, fruits, and meat. Apples were, and continue to be, an important part of the agricultural heritage of the town, with many orchardists in the area, including Sweetser's Apple Barrel and Orchards dating to 1812, and the Double T Orchard, founded by the Terison brothers in the 1950s in West Cumberland. Poultry farming had become one of the leading industries by 1900, with at least three main poultry dealers and processors in town, who sent their product to the urban markets by express rail shipment through Cumberland Junction. In West Cumberland, Mel Wilson shipped birds and chicks to Portland and Lewiston on the Portland-Lewiston Interurban. The workers processing the birds were mostly female. In the early 1890s, Frank and Arno Chase had a greenhouse in Cumberland and sold flowers under the Chase Brothers name. By 1904, the town had four large greenhouses boasting 28,000 feet of glass, producing primarily carnations for the state's wholesale trade. During the 1920s, Howard C. Blanchard constructed two large houses with 30,000 square feet of glass. Just as with the town's poultry businesses, the proprietors of Cumberland's flower operations depended on the 40 trains a day that passed through Cumberland Junction, some of them providing express service to Bangor, Portland, Boston, and New York. Another relatively recent endeavor in town in the early 1900s was trout farming, and the Roland and Rowe's ponds were said to be stocked with in excess of 5,000 fish. Dairy farming and beef cattle were also mainstays of the area's farms, including Broadmoor and Spring Brook farms. Spring Brook and Sweetser's Apple Barrel are two of the long-running local farms still in business, while the Cumberland Farmer's Market runs every summer from May to October and the Cumberland County Fair is held annually in the fall.

HORSE TRACKS AT THE CUMBERLAND FAIR. Each year during the third week of September, thousands of people flock to the intersection of Blanchard and Bruce Hill Roads for the Cumberland Fair. Presented by the Cumberland Farmers Club at the Cumberland Fairgrounds, 2019 saw the 148th edition of the event that started as the Cumberland Center Fair. The harness racing that now occurs on a standard track at the fairgrounds once took place on Main Street, which also was the site of the ox pulling and other events. In addition, the meetinghouse sheds were filled with hogs, colts, sheep, oxen, steers, cows, and other livestock for display. Activities included horse races and a luncheon with food prepared from a local kitchen. Lacking a building, many families brought picnic lunches and ate under tents.

CUMBERLAND FAIR TRADE CARD, 1887. Solomon Loring Blanchard, in a letter to his brother, recalls the 1871 fair: "About 9 o'clock people began to come and by noon Cumberland Center seemed like Tremont Street, Boston. It was the largest assembly of people Cumberland ever had. The Town House was filled with articles of agriculture and fancy work and was a splendid sight to behold." Following the success of the fair, it became apparent the town needed a hall big enough to host exhibitions, and the fair was moved from Cumberland Center to West Cumberland in 1875, although not without controversy and acrimony. Trade cards advertising the 1887 Cumberland Fair featured whimsical, nature-inspired illustrations of young girls. Currently, the fair features seven full days of livestock exhibits and competitions, an exhibition hall, the annual Maine State Pumpkin and Squash Weigh-in contest, tours of the Farm Museum, midway rides, and competitions in art, photography, baking, canned goods, crafts, needlework, and other categories.

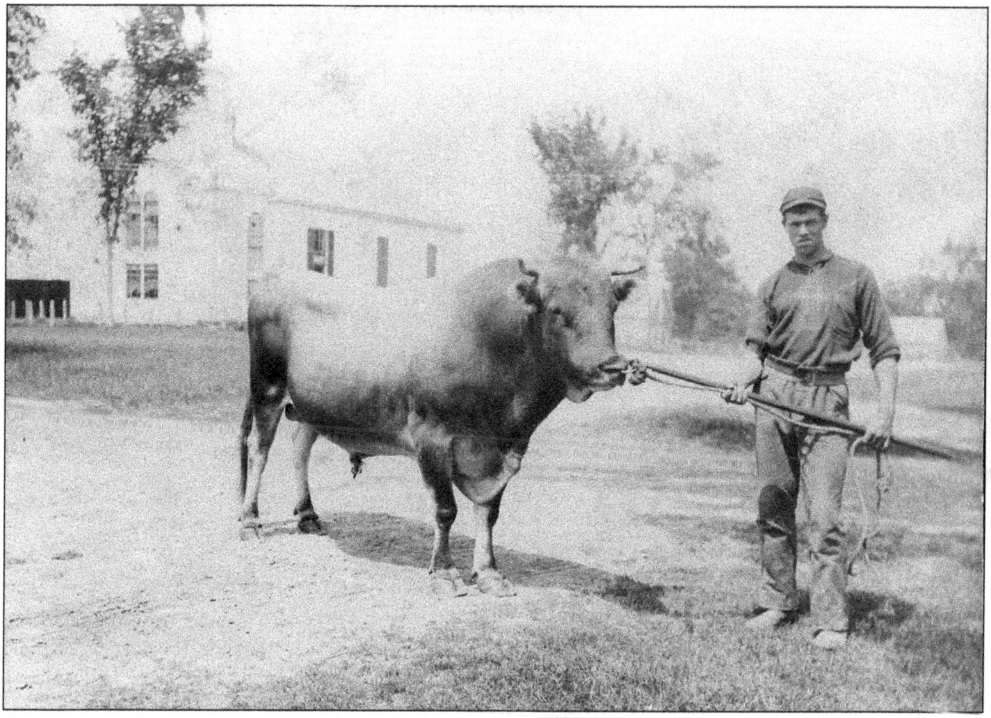

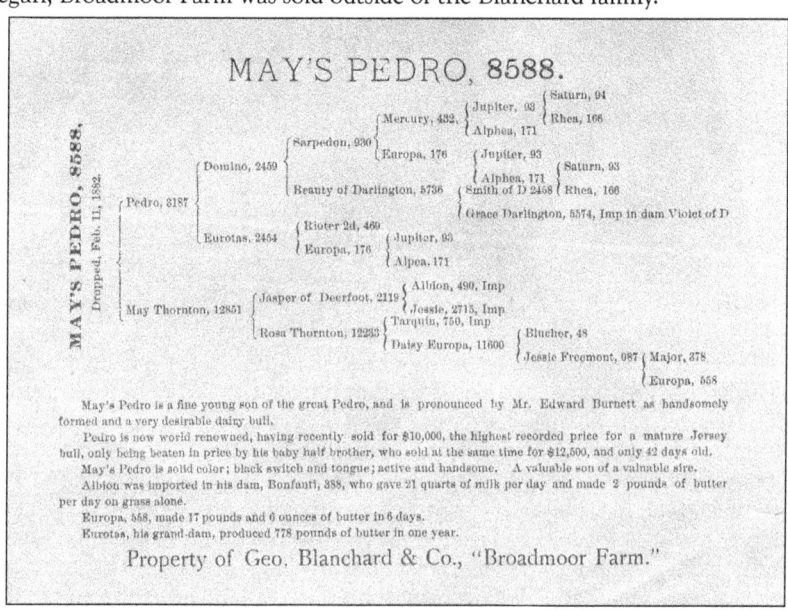

Broadmoor Farm. In 1829, Nathaniel Blanchard bought the land at the corner of Main Street and Tuttle Road from Joel Prince. His son Capt. Enos Blanchard took over the farm in 1833, and his wife, Joanna, managed it while he was away at sea. In 1874, their son George (seen above) started the Broadmoor Farm with purebred Jersey cattle, which became widely famous throughout the United States and sold for as much as $1,500. Many earned the highest honors from the American Jersey Cattle Club. In 1935, the farm passed to George's son Arthur Blanchard, who continued the business of selling quality cattle until his death in 1972. In 1974, a hundred years after it began, Broadmoor Farm was sold outside of the Blanchard family.

MAY'S PEDRO, 8588.

MAY'S PEDRO, 8588.
Dropped, Feb. 11, 1882.

Pedro, 3187
Domino, 2459
Sarpedon, 930
Mercury, 432,
Jupiter, 93
Saturn, 94
Rhea, 166
Alphea, 171
Europa, 176
Beauty of Darlington, 5736
Jupiter, 93
Alphea, 171
Smith of D 2458
Saturn, 93
Rhea, 166
Grace Darlington, 5574, Imp in dam Violet of D
Eurotas, 2454
Rioter 2d, 469
Europa, 176
Jupiter, 93
Alpea, 171
May Thornton, 12851
Jasper of Deerfoot, 2119
Albion, 490, Imp
Jessie, 2715, Imp
Rosa Thornton, 12233
Tarquin, 750, Imp
Daisy Europa, 11600
Blucher, 48
Jessie Freemont, 087
Major, 378
Europa, 558

May's Pedro is a fine young son of the great Pedro, and is pronounced by Mr. Edward Burnett as handsomely formed and a very desirable dairy bull.

Pedro is now world renowned, having recently sold for $10,000, the highest recorded price for a mature Jersey bull, only being beaten in price by his baby half brother, who sold at the same time for $12,500, and only 42 days old.

May's Pedro is solid color; black switch and tongue; active and handsome. A valuable son of a valuable sire.

Albion was imported in his dam, Bonfanti, 388, who gave 21 quarts of milk per day and made 2 pounds of butter per day on grass alone.

Europa, 558, made 17 pounds and 6 ounces of butter in 6 days.

Eurotas, his grand-dam, produced 778 pounds of butter in one year.

Property of Geo. Blanchard & Co., "Broadmoor Farm."

WILSON FARM, WEST CUMBERLAND. Wilson Farm in West Cumberland was established in 1812 when Cyrus H. Wilson raised the farm's main barn. Mel and Mabel Wilson took over the farm in the 1920s and turned it into one of the biggest poultry operations in Maine, hatching up to 250,000 chicks per season. The photograph to the right shows Mel Wilson with one of his birds. Their son Jimmy started a dairy operation at the farm after purchasing a purebred Jersey heifer from Arthur Blanchard in 1939. The Wilson barn burned in 1974, followed by a ruptured milk tank in 1975 and a collapse of the new barn's roof. Mel and Mabel abandoned the farming life in 1977. (Both, courtesy of Lynda Jensen.)

BURGESS POULTRY FARM. By 1900, poultry farming was one of the leading industries in Cumberland, with the principal breeds being White Wyandottes, Plymouth Rocks, and Rhode Island Reds. An average poultry business in the area, like the Shaw Brothers in West Cumberland, wintered about 600 hens and hatched from 1,000 to 2,000 chicks each season. Eggs were also shipped for hatching. There were at least three main poultry dealers and processors in town whose product was processed, packed in ice, and shipped to Boston and other urban markets by express rail shipment through Cumberland Junction. George Burgess and his wife lived on one such poultry farm (seen here), with living quarters in the two-story central structure and chickens in the two wings. In 1966, the Burgess farm was burned during a fire department training exercise and became the site for the new Mabel I. Wilson School.

CORN-SHOP. The corn-shop, a canning factory at Cumberland Junction, was established in 1881 by Merrill Brothers. Initially, Merrill Brothers produced their own tin cans but later outsourced cans from a Massachusetts-based company and focused on canning. The cans were wrapped with brightly illustrated labels, like the one seen below, and shipped by boxcar. The canning factory was sold to William R. Wood of Portland, who was proprietor in 1904 and ran the business as United Packers, with a capacity of 3,000 cans per day. Corn was canned extensively, with other vegetables and fruit also handled. While under the management of Merrill Brothers, meat was also canned. Charles E. Herrick and his son Horatio operated a second corn-canning factory in the late 1890s that provided seasonal employment for many of the town's young people.

SWEETSER ORCHARDS. Sweetser's Apple Barrel and Orchards began as a family homestead built in 1812 for Mary Ann Pittee, whose daughter Mary Jane Pittee married Samuel Robinson Sweetser. During the mid-1800s, a thriving apple orchard covered the 14-acre farm property, which was passed down through the generations from Samuel and Mary Jane, to Frederick and Mary Eliza Sweetser, to Herman and Phyllis Sweetser, to Dick and Connie Sweetser, and currently, to their son Greg Sweetser. Several apple trees from the 1800s still produce heirloom Wolf River and Northern Spy varieties. Frederick Sweetser diversified the farm through a very successful meat-packing business and was an early member of the Maine Pomological Society. His son Herman was a professor of horticulture at the University of Maine at Orono who returned to Cumberland in 1926 to run the family orchard. During the mid-to-late 1900s, five major orchards were active in Cumberland. Today, only Terison Apple Orchard and Sweetser's Apple Barrel and Orchards remain. Other orchardists in the area included George Emery and Arthur Blanchard. Above, Frederick Sweetser poses with his oxen; below, Herman Sweetser sorts apples. (Both, courtesy of Dick and Connie Sweetser.)

Lenville Hawkes, Washington, DC. Another important crop in Maine is the potato. In 1931, Lenville Hawkes of West Cumberland delivered 40 bushels of Maine potatoes to Pres. Herbert Hoover using a two-wheeled cart pulled by a pair of Hereford-Durham oxen. The gift was a joint effort by Maine governor William Tudor Gardiner, the Potato Committee of New England Shippers' Advisory Board, the Maine State Agricultural Department, and the Maine Development Commission, and was designed to bring the Maine potato crop to the attention of the American public. These photographs were taken on November 23, 1931, and show Hawkes in front of the US Capitol and his cart at the White House.

FRANK CHASE HOME AND GREENHOUSE. Cumberland was once known as the carnation capital of the country. At one time, there were four greenhouse ranges in Cumberland: the two Chase brothers, Charles Jenkins, and Howard Blanchard's Sunnyside. Frank and Arno Chase sold plants from a wagon with the name Chase Brothers painted on the side, and around 1892, had a greenhouse at 273 Tuttle Road. In 1896, Arno built his own greenhouse, while Frank remained at the Chase homestead until 1915, when his greenhouse burned. Frank Chase moved to Main Street and built a new greenhouse (pictured) at 327 Main Street. When he died in 1933, his widow, Geneva Chase, assumed responsibility for the business. The small building with the tall chimney between the residence and greenhouse was where the heat for the greenhouse was generated. (Courtesy of Phil Chase.)

ARNO CHASE DELIVERY WAGON AND GREENHOUSE. After moving his greenhouse to the corner of Main Street and Tuttle Road in Cumberland Center, Arno Chase continued to deliver carnations in a horse-drawn wagon painted Chase Brothers. In the above photograph, dated about 1910, Chase holds the reins and his daughter Laura sits beside him. After receiving orders from New York, New Jersey, and Boston, he would pick carnations, take them to the cool cellar of his workshop, separate them into groups of 25, wrap them carefully in tissue paper, put them in boxes, and deliver to Cumberland Junction in time for the 4:00 p.m. southbound train. He raised four kinds of heirloom carnations with vivid colors and expansive blooms. Altogether, Arno Chase erected three small greenhouses, giving him 10,000 square feet of glass. (Both, courtesy of Phil Chase.)

ARNO CHASE GREENHOUSE AFTER FIRE. In March 1933, one of Arno Chase's greenhouses caught fire. "[A] large crowd gathered at the Congregational Church to hear Donald MacMillan lecture and show pictures of his trip to the Arctic. The fire alarm blew, and the male members of the audience disappeared to help fight the fire at Arno Chase's," Barbara Blanchard Garsoe recalled. "It was very dark, but seeing the glow in the sky kept us going. It looked as if the whole town were on fire." Luckily, the fire did not spread, and Chase rebuilt and remained in business until about 1940. Howard Blanchard also grew carnations, and in the 1920s erected two large houses of 30,000 square feet, including the second-largest greenhouse in Maine. Local markets were expanding, and by 1960, the entire crop was distributed in Maine and New Hampshire. In time, however, entrepreneurs in Latin American countries began growing carnations in their naturally warmer climates and delivering them to US southern ports at lower prices, and Cumberland's carnation business dwindled. (Courtesy of Phil Chase.)

Five

OVERSEERS OF THE POOR

The Cumberland Overseers of the Poor was the municipal board created under the authority of the so-called pauper laws, which were passed by the Maine legislature in March 1821 and governed the treatment of the state's poor and indigent citizens. The state's mandate to its municipalities to provide for the support of their poor residents was a continuation of the laws Maine inherited from Massachusetts, which in turn were linked directly to England's 1601 Poor Law Act and 1662 Settlement Laws. Maine's pauper laws remained in effect until the mid-1970s. The law stated that legal settlement in a municipality was gained by birth or marriage, through warrant at a legal meeting, by living in an unincorporated place when it became incorporated, or through legal settlement in a town that was divided. Minors could gain settlement by serving an apprenticeship for four years in a town and setting up lawful trade within one year of the expiration of their term, while individuals over 21 could gain settlement by residing in a town for five years without receiving support as a pauper. Once legal settlement was established for an individual, a municipality was required to provide relief for those in need, while the person's relatives were obligated to contribute to their support in proportion to their ability to do so. Relief could be of two general types: "outdoor" relief or aid in the form of food, clothing, and boarding in a private home, and "indoor" relief, where a person resided in an almshouse, workhouse, or town farm. Postrevolutionary America questioned the traditional colonial system of providing outdoor relief because it was a community responsibility, and poverty came to be seen as a social problem that should be targeted for reform. A less-tolerant view toward long-term dependence led towns and cities nationwide to build almshouses for their poor during the 1820s and 1830s. In theory, almshouses used hygiene, discipline, routine, and work to transform the poor into valuable and industrious members of society, although the reality in Maine presented a more complicated tableau of poverty, mental illness, and inequality.

PAUPER AUCTION AT TOWN MEETING. One method used to secure outdoor relief for paupers was to bid them off at town meeting. This document from May 1831 shows the pauper's name in the column on the left, the amount agreed upon for services, and the name of the person agreeing to provide care. In this document, William Thompson agrees to board William Noyes in his house in return for $2. per week.

INDENTURE OF DAVID WEBBER. Minors who were chargeable to the town could be contracted out as indentured apprentices. Boys could be indentured until they turned 21, and girls were indentured until they turned 18 or married. In exchange, boys and girls received instruction in reading and writing, and boys in math. This June 1830 indenture placed six-year-old David Webber into an apprenticeship with his uncle, who was to teach him "the art, trade, or mystery of a Husbandman."

TOWN FARM ON BROAD COVE. On April 3, 1837, Cumberland voters approved the purchase of "a suitable farm on which to keep and maintain the paupers belonging to this town." Cumberland's first town farm was on the Foreside, near Spear's shipyard and the shores of Broad Cove. A receipt for supplies for the town farm for May to December 1843 includes 1,453 pounds of oakum, a loose fiber obtained by recycling old rope and cordage that was mixed with tar and used for caulking in shipbuilding. Picking oakum was a common task in British workhouses and penitentiaries, and possibly orphanages. Its presence at Cumberland's town farm indicates that the farm's inhabitants were engaged in work, probably for the nearby shipyard, that offset the cost of maintaining the farm. (Both, courtesy of Almira Cram Willson.)

TOWN FARM EXPENSES AND SAVINGS. In addition to picking oakum, the town farm itself was a way for Cumberland to recoup expenses. According to the 1855 overseer's report, the residents of the town farm, under the guidance of overseer E.S. Duran, produced 10 tons of hay, 75 bushels of corn, 290 bushels of potatoes, 13 bushels of wheat, 8 bushels each of beans and beets, and 25 bushels of apples. The stock on the farm consisted of a yoke of oxen, 4 cows, and 14 sheep. Supplies on hand included 200 pounds of beef, 300 pounds of pork, 35 pounds of bacon, 30 pounds of butter, 45 pounds of dried apples, and 40 cords of wood, and expenditures for other items were minimal. Indoor relief resulted in considerable savings for the town. (Both, courtesy of Almira Cram Willson.)

DECLINE OF INDOOR RELIEF. On February 26, 1866, Cumberland voters approved a measure to "sell the Town Farm and all the appurtenances thereof." According to the 1865 overseer's report, in "regard to the Paupers now in the almshouse . . . death has swept them away & but one remains as a living monument to mark the house as an almshouse. On the 19th inst. Lemuel Hamilton died, he was found dead, having fallen into the fire & burned to death. Emery Gould ran away a few weeks since and has not been heard from." Cumberland closed its almshouse apparently due to lack of residents; at the same time, communities across the country were shuttering their town farms and almshouses thanks to the efforts of Dorothea Dix, a Maine native and social reformer who traveled the country in the 1840s documenting the often meager or abusive conditions of prisoners and poorhouse residents. (Courtesy of Almira Cram Willson.)

Town Farm on Blanchard Road. After Cumberland closed its almshouse in 1866, the town again relied on outdoor relief for several years. In 1888, it purchased the former James A. Blanchard farm on Blanchard Road for a second town farm and almshouse. The town's reestablishment of an indoor relief system, after two decades of an ever-increasing financial burden in providing for the town's poor, indicates that the financial benefits of indoor relief outweighed the negative aspects of the system. The Blanchard Road almshouse was sold on May 23, 1904, nearly three years after the death of Olive Titcomb, its last resident. Outside support, specifically boarding a person in a private home, was approved by the town, and the economical town-farm system was superseded by the need for specialized care for the mentally ill and the voters' estimation of how the poor should be supported. From 1900 to 1911, the town spent $8,017 on outside support; of that amount, 65 percent was paid to the Maine Insane Hospital in Augusta for the board and care of a handful of individuals.

CRAM FAMILY ON THE DALTON FARM. After leaving the care of the Overseers of the Poor, the first town farm's land passed through several hands. Ephraim Sturdivant bought the property from the Town of Cumberland in 1866 for $1,900; his widow, Mary Sturdivant, sold it to Albert Drinkwater in 1869. Drinkwater and his brother Joseph sold it to Maria Dalton in 1873. Linwood and Gertrude Cram, who lived there with their children Robert, Marshall, Elton, and Lydia, rented the farm from Dalton from at least 1904 through 1919. In a 1986 interview, Robert Cram recalls, "[W]e lived there to keep the farm going and probably did whatever they did in the summer." The photograph below shows Robert H. Cram haying on the Dalton farm, sometime around 1910. (Both, courtesy of Almira Cram Willson.)

DALTON COTTAGE. The photograph at left shows the Dalton cottage on the farm, where Edith Dalton frequently stayed. Cram recalls that her mother "could have bought that whole farm for $1,800. They offered it to her for $1,800, 110 acres and the old house. But . . . you never could think of getting that much money in your whole life." In 1920, Herbert J. Brown bought the land, and by 1938, the Payson family had inherited it. After the death of Merrill Payson Robbins in 2012, the Payson heirs sold 104 acres, including the house, valued at over $2 million dollars, to land developers Bateman, Bateman, and Anastos, who converted the land into 10 luxury ocean-view plots, a stark transformation from its early days as a pauper farm. (Both, courtesy of Almira Cram Willson.)

Six

FIRE DEPARTMENTS

The early days of fire protection in Cumberland relied on a bucket brigade volunteer system. However, households were often far apart, and reliable access to volunteers and water was not always possible. Cumberland experimented with a variety of firefighting tactics, and as early as the 1910s slowly began to build up an arsenal of firefighting equipment, including hoses, improvised fire trucks, fire extinguishers, hydrants, and a crew of volunteer firefighters. In 1915, Portland firefighter Lester B. Bragg became the first fire chief of Cumberland, although when the position was established, it was in title only, as there was little equipment, no department, no budget, and no organized manpower. In the 1920s, Cumberland made major advancements in its firefighting practices. After Bragg's death in 1921, Gilbert Strout became fire chief, and the town purchased its first truck, a used Model T Ford that cost $1,400, which was housed in a stable on Main Street. By 1928, a group of 18 men had formed the town's first official fire company under Chief Strout, complete with officers and bylaws. As the town's needs evolved, the Cumberland Fire Department evolved with it, working to keep safety equipment current, and building, renovating, and rebuilding stations. Three fire stations were established in Cumberland Center, West Cumberland, and on Chebeague Island in an effort to make the department's reach as wide and responsive as possible. In response to firefighter needs, volunteer organizations like the Red Network in 1953 and the Ladies' Auxiliary in 1970 arose to support the department. Today, a far cry from its humble and necessary beginnings in community garages and local kitchens, the Cumberland Fire Department serves the entire town of Cumberland and provides mutual aid for surrounding towns during major emergencies.

OLD CENTRAL STATION. In an effort to efficiently combat local fires prior to the creation of a formal fire department, Cumberland experimented with a combination of new firefighting tactics. In 1912, before it owned a fire truck, the town purchased a 35-gallon chemical reversible tank, mounted on wheels and drawn by manpower; in 1913, the town acquired hand fire extinguishers; and in 1914, the town voted to fix the price of labor for firefighters. Lester B. Bragg, a firefighter at the India Street Station in Portland, served as Cumberland's first official fire chief from 1915 until his death in 1921. Cumberland's first fire station was a one-bay metal building beside the old blacksmith's shop, built in 1921 for $340. In 1928, the town bought a new truck and converted half of the town hall into a fire station. The newly formed Cumberland Center Water Company strategically placed small hydrants throughout Cumberland Center.

FORD V-8 FIRETRUCK, 1936. In 1936, the Town of Cumberland purchased its first brand-new fire truck, a Ford V-8 with a built-in pump and ladders, from the McCann Truck Company in Portland. The Cumberland Town Hall was subsequently remodeled to hold all the town-owned vehicles: one fire truck, one snowplow, and one school bus. The new engine remained in service until 1961 and remains a parade vehicle today. Above, the children of Fire Chief Kenneth Chase, Philip and Barbara, pose in the 1936 truck. Philip Chase would become Cumberland's fire chief in 1966. In 1936, the fire department also built a fire pond off Main Street for better water supply in Cumberland Center. (Both, courtesy of Phil Chase.)

West Cumberland Fire Station. Residents in West Cumberland felt a need for quicker emergency services in their neighborhood. In 1942, at no cost to the town, West Cumberland volunteers built their own fire station on donated land on Blackstrap Road and raised money for a truck and resuscitator for near-drownings at Forest Lake. In 1962, they relocated to a one-bay station on Blackstrap Road. At a dramatic 1964 town meeting, the townspeople decided by a one-vote margin to build a new West Cumberland Fire Station from scratch instead of upgrading the old one. The budget committee and town officials had opposed the appropriation because they said they did not feel it was absolutely necessary, although Fire Chief Harold M. Bragg noted the majority of the volunteer firemen available during the day lived in the West Cumberland area. For the $13,500 appropriated, the new station included a heating system, a hard-top driveway, an artesian well, and water piped into the station. Volunteer work by the firemen in West Cumberland helped hold down the cost.

CHEBEAGUE ISLAND FIRE STATIONS, OLD AND NEW. The Chebeague Island Fire Department was part of the Cumberland Fire Department until the island established itself as a separate town in 2007. Chebeague received its first fire truck in 1928, which was housed near the Island Hall; prior to the truck, nearly every major fire on the island was considered a total loss. In 1947, an out-of-control fire burned through dry evergreens on the island for two days, destroying two and a half acres. Following this fire, Cumberland recognized the importance of equipping Chebeague's fire department since other departments were not able to respond during a major disaster. The photograph above shows Chebeague's old three-bay fire station; below is the current station.

THE SUMMONING SYSTEM. The methods of summoning help in the event of a fire have changed over the years. Around 1932, a siren was placed on top of the town hall, the site of the current Central Fire Station. The button to operate the siren was installed in the telephone office, which was around the corner at 281 Main Street. When a fire was reported, a call went to the telephone office, and the operator activated the siren; there would be a continuous three-ring on each party line to alert people to the fire. As a boy, Fire Chief Harold Bragg remembered turning a hand generator to get enough power to keep up the alarm.

THE RED NETWORK AND LADIES' AUXILIARY. With the arrival of a dial system in 1952, the Red Network replaced the telephone operator. Several special telephones were installed in firemen's homes, and it often fell to the firemen's wives to respond and notify the firemen of fires. This system continued until 1966, when the department acquired a full-time operator and airhorn system to summon firefighters. Under the new system, a call to the Cumberland Fire Department would scramble the operators, who each had a list of eight to twelve firefighters to alert. The 1966 Red Network members pictured here are, from left to right, (seated) Doris Leland, Elsie Burnell, Helen Bragg, and Marion Small; (standing) Ella White, Evelyn Chase, Mabel Slusser, Barbara Garsoe, Rebecca Maloney, Janet Bragg, Connie Sweetser, and Betty Reardon. Another organization, the Ladies' Auxiliary, was formalized in 1970 as a way to supply the fire department with provisions during large emergency situations, although it existed informally long before this.

CUMBERLAND RESCUE. Cumberland Rescue began in 1958, with a used blue panel truck acquired as government surplus from Dow Air Force Base in Bangor and local citizens who trained as emergency medical service personnel. A 1971 fund drive enabled the fire department to purchase the first vehicle that was actually built as an ambulance and outfitted with tools and equipment for rescue work. In 1991, Cumberland Rescue was temporarily divorced from the fire department and operated as an independent organization, but they were reunified in 2009. Today, the rescue service remains an integral part of the fire department. In the above photograph are, from left to right, Dick Sweetser, Edward "Ned" Bragg, and Phil Chase. Below, from left to right, Ned Bragg, Phil Chase, George Small, John Crandall, Francis Small, unidentified, and Dick Sweetser pose at the old Central Station. (Both, courtesy of Phil Chase.)

CUMBERLAND FIRE CHIEFS AND THE NEW CENTRAL STATION. In 1965, five fire chiefs stand in front of the former Central Fire Station as it burns to make room to build the new Central Station, below, on Tuttle Road. From left to right are Maurice Small, Phil Chase, Harold Bragg, Kenneth Chase, and Edward Bragg. Renovations to improve Central Station began in 2016. It retained four bays, but the office section to the left was demolished and a three-story addition built in its place. This new and improved facility, dedicated on May 12, 2018, contains living quarters on the third floor, a small conference room, a 50-person community room complete with a full kitchen, and offices for the chief and other officers. (Both, courtesy of Phil Chase.)

CONTROLLED BURN OF BURGESS FARM. When poultry farmer George Burgess retired in 1965, he sold his home, business, and land on Tuttle Road to the school district to build what is now the Mabel I. Wilson School. To clear the site for construction of the new school, the fire department demolished the buildings with a controlled burn as a training program for firefighters. Today, the Cumberland Fire Department is part of the Coastal Mutual Aid Association and is prepared to provide aid for a number of neighboring towns in the event of a major emergency.

Seven
LIBRARIES

Prior to a brick-and-mortar building, Cumberland's libraries relied on subscriptions, volunteer librarians, and private homes to allow people in the community access to books. In 1747, Deacon John White of the First Congregational Church of North Yarmouth left a bequest that helped establish a lending library near the church. In December 1793, just prior to the founding of the Second Congregational Church of North Yarmouth, 40 men and one woman established the Second Social Library in North Yarmouth, in the village that would later become Cumberland Center. The Second Social Library in North Yarmouth was incorporated in 1817, and with the secession of Cumberland from North Yarmouth in 1821, became the First Social Library of Cumberland. In 1897, Rev. Frank Davis, pastor of the Congregational Church in Cumberland from 1892 to 1899, and his wife, Helen, organized a network of volunteer librarians who managed what became known as the Cumberland Library. The books of the Cumberland Library were housed in the homes of its volunteer librarians, and titles were added in accordance with community interests. The deaths of Carroll D. and Annie Lincoln Prince in late 1920 resulted in a bequest of $35,000 for the construction of a public library in Carroll's birthplace of Cumberland. Prince Memorial Library was incorporated on November 7, 1921, and the following February was granted a plot of land on Main Street. Construction of the new library took place in 1922. The original brick building, designed by architect George Chase Emery, opened to the public on January 7, 1923. Prince Memorial Library has had three additions over the years: the Merrill Addition, completed in 1959; the Cumberland Wing, dedicated on October 1, 1987; and the Young Adult Room, dedicated on April 3, 1996. Today, the library's collection houses more than 54,000 items.

SECOND SOCIAL LIBRARY OF NORTH YARMOUTH. By 1780, there were at least 50 social libraries in New England. The Second Social Library of North Yarmouth joined that group when it was founded in December 1793. The library was incorporated on January 13, 1817, and became the First Social Library of Cumberland after the town seceded in 1821. The surviving record book indicates that most books were volumes of sermons and other religious texts, with some historical volumes interspersed. A proprietor could buy a share of the library for $2, allowing them to borrow one book at a time for up to two months, and overdue books were charged 1¢ a day. The last entry in the record book is dated March 30, 1855, and was a call to subscribers to see what disposition would be made of the books.

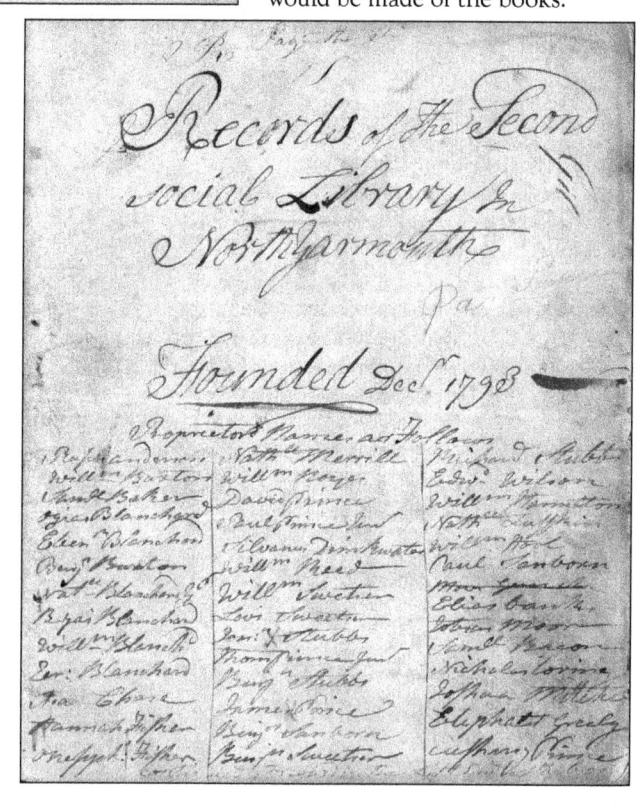

1897.

Catalogue OF CUMBERLAND LIBRARY.

1.	Standish of Standish.	Jane G. Austen
2.	Betty Alden.	" "
3.	Dr. LeBaron and His Daughters.	" "
4.	A Nameless Nobleman.	" "
~~5.~~	~~A New England Nun~~, etc.	Mary E. Wilkins
~~6.~~	~~Feeding Animals~~.	Elliott M. Stewart
7.	Robert Falconer.	Geo. MacDonald
8.	Shirley.	Charlotte Bronte
9.	Hypatia.	Charles Kingsley
10.	How the Farm Pays.	W. Croziers P. Henderson
~~11.~~	~~Drone's Honey.~~	Sophie May
12.	The Story of the Normans.	Sarah Orne Jewett
~~13.~~	~~Gardening for Profit~~.	Peter Henderson
~~14.~~	~~Our Farming~~.	T. B. Terry
15.	Friend Olivia.	Amelia E. Barr
16.	Uarda.	George Ebers
17.	A Noble Life.	Dinah M. Craik
~~18.~~	~~Prince of India.~~ Vol. I.	Gen. Lew Wallace
~~19.~~	~~Prince of India.~~ Vol. II.	" "
~~20.~~	~~The Last of the Barons.~~	Sir Edward B. Lytton
21.	Ramona.	Helen Hunt Jackson
22.	A Man without a Country.	Edward E. Hale
~~23.~~	~~Fruit Culture~~.	W. E. Strong
24.	The War of Independence.	John Fiske
25.	Louisa May Alcott.	Edna D. Cheney
26.	Doctor Zay.	Elizabeth S. Phelps
27.	A Country Doctor.	Sarah Orne Jewett
~~28.~~	~~A Tillyloss Scandal~~.	J. M. Barrie
~~29.~~	~~What I know of Farming.~~	Horace Greeley

Cumberland Library Catalogue and Cora Adams House. In 1897, Rev. Frank Davis, pastor of the Congregational Church of Cumberland from 1892 to 1899, and his wife, Helen, were instrumental in organizing the Cumberland Library, which was housed and managed by volunteer librarians, including Annie Buxton Small, Cora Adams (who lived in the house below with her husband, blacksmith Fred Adams), Esther Hill, and Olive M. Hall. Books were kept in various households, and subscribers had their own personal catalogs, consisting of 10.5-by-14.7-centimeter cardstock printed front and back, with two punch holes so they could be tied together with string. Each card listed the titles and authors of around 70 books, and new cards were printed as each new batch of books was added.

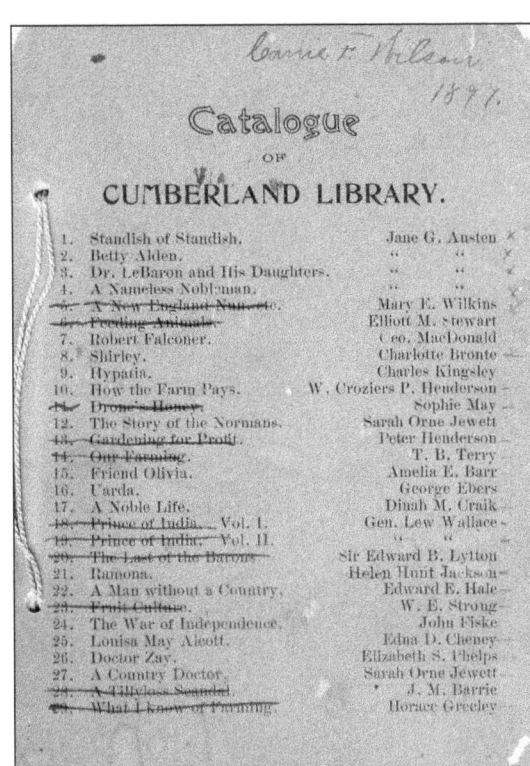

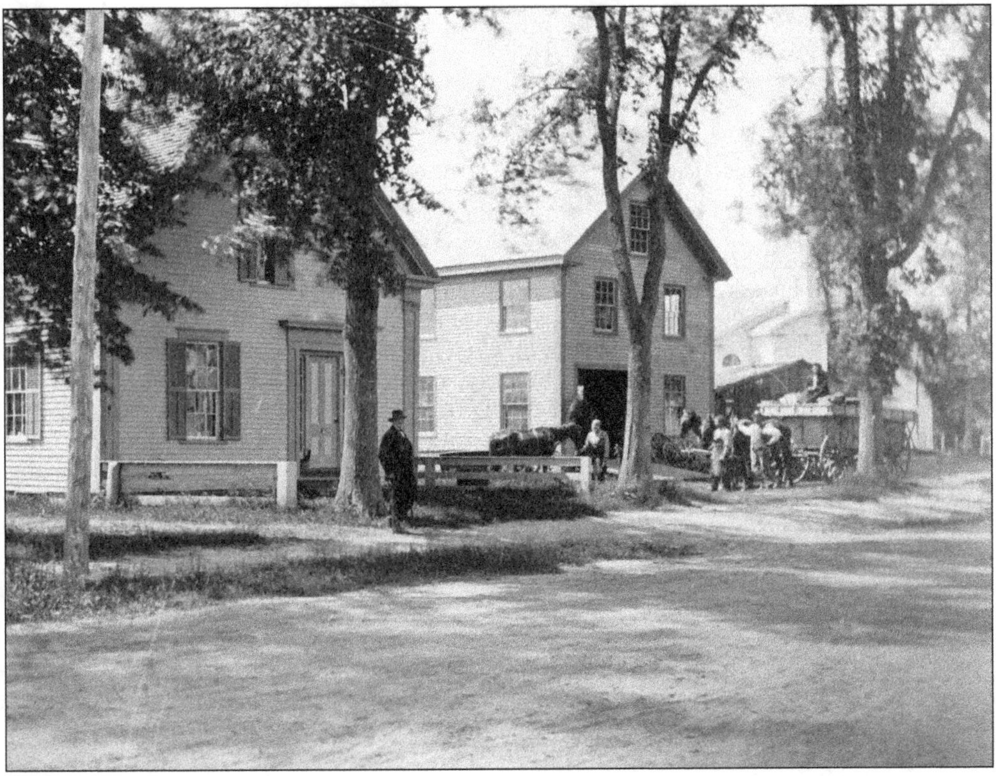

THE CUMBERLAND LIBRARY: OLIVE HALL. As the library was largely organized and run by women, the titles often reflected the interests of the women at the time, mostly fiction from the late 1800s and early 1900s, with no reference books or children's books at all. By 1921, the printed catalog included 675 titles, including biographies, histories, and novels. The Cumberland Library's last location was the home of Olive Hall at 283 Main Street. Hall, a widow, lived with her daughter and son-in-law Arno Chase in a two-family house, and Chase recalls two rooms of shelves filled with books, each with a number on the spine and in new condition with a paper cover, no matter how long it had been in the library. Mildred Doane remembers "the smell of books and a kerosene lamp at Mrs. Hall's. . . . It was a great event when we heard that new books were in."

CONSTRUCTION OF PRINCE MEMORIAL LIBRARY. In 1920, the deaths of Carroll D. and Annie L. Prince just six weeks apart resulted in a $35,000 bequest to construct a public library for Carroll's hometown. In November 1921, Prince Memorial Library was incorporated due to their largesse. Maud Merrill Thomes donated a four-acre parcel on Main Street for the library, and construction began in 1922. Prince Memorial Library opened to the public on January 7, 1923, with over 600 books from the earlier Cumberland Library on the shelves. According to the *Maine Sunday Telegram*, the building was "of very attractive design, of the simple colonial style, constructed of water struck brick, with Hallowell granite trimmings and roof of slate." George Chase Emery of Waltham, Massachusetts, was the architect, and contractor F.A. Rummery of Portland built the library.

THE LEGEND OF GRANNY BANKS. One local Cumberland legend involves Granny Banks, who lived in a shack near the southwest corner of the Prince Memorial Library lot and was believed to be a witch. Margaret Wyman, recalling the stories of her uncle Horatio Herrick, colorfully describes Granny Banks as "tall and straight as an arrow with piercing black eyes, jet black hair, and a set of teeth she could have sold to princesses for their weight in diamonds. . . . Her toothpicks were always the splinters from a lightning riven tree." Wyman attributes several stories of mischief and local inconvenience to Granny Banks, including summoning a horde of hogs and eerily silent dogs on those who had annoyed her, bewitching lye to not form into soap, eating snakes, and even transforming into a skunk. According to Wyman, the only person Granny Banks cared for was Sophia Smith, the parson's wife.

PRINCE MEMORIAL LIBRARY INTERIOR. These images show the interior of Prince Memorial Library shortly after it opened in 1921. By that time, there were 113 public libraries in Maine, compared to only 15 in the 1880s. The period after the Civil War saw an accumulation of surplus wealth, and portions of that wealth drove the growth of libraries in Maine through gifts and bequests. In addition to housing circulating collections of books, the state's public libraries often became cultural centers and repositories for special book and art collections. Many of the new public libraries replaced existing social libraries, and libraries in general were seen as serving the educational needs of adults. Some advocated for libraries to collect and archive local history, biographies, and anything else relating to their communities.

MERRILL ADDITION. By the 1950s, the library needed additional space. Paul E. Merrill, son of Wallace L. and Harriet Merrill, whose mother was one of the original library corporators and served for 35 years as chairman of the book committee as well as interim librarian, made a gift to the town of an addition to the library in memory of his parents. During the summer of 1959, excavation was started for a 40-by-20-foot addition to the rear of Prince Memorial Library to be built by contractor Clifford L. Weeks. The original building was redecorated, a new heating plant was installed, and rooms in the basement were set aside for office space and a community meeting room. The Merrill Addition opened in November 1959. In 1980, Paul Merrill had plans drawn up for a museum dedicated to Cumberland's history, to be situated on library grounds. The plan never came to fruition.

LIBRARY CORPORATION. At the request of the Library Corporation, in 1968, the town voted to assume the assets and responsibilities of the library. Funds from the original bequest, after the construction of the building in 1922, were, by 1925, insufficient to maintain and operate the facility. The town began contributing to its support, and by 1966 was supplying all but one-ninth of its expenses. Bylaws were changed to make the five selectmen members of the Board of Corporators having a majority vote, although all officers of the corporation were to be elected from the four members of the board who were not selectmen. The town treasurer served as treasurer of the library corporation. A reception was held honoring the outgoing trustees, one of whom was Harlan H. Sweetser, one of the original corporators who had been president of the corporation for 37 years.

CHILDREN'S ROOM. Use of the library continued to grow, and it became necessary to ask the Cumberland Historical Society, which had been using the meeting room in the basement, to find new quarters. In 1972, a children's library section was located in that basement room, and Ellen Albin was the named children's librarian. The Town of North Yarmouth, whose residents used Cumberland's library, began contributing to its support. In 1982, the library corporation bylaws were again amended to make Prince Memorial Library a department within town government under the direct supervision of the town manager. By 1984, the library was open five days a week, and the librarian, assistant librarian, and children's librarian were all full-time employees. Head librarians at Prince Memorial Library over the years include Cecil W. Adams, who served from 1923 to 1930; Harriet C. Merrill, chairman of the book committee and interim librarian; Mildred W. Doane, who was appointed librarian in June 1931; and Phyllis S. Sweetser, the librarian from 1951 to 1970, when Martha B. Pawle was appointed.

CUMBERLAND WING. In 1985, Cumberland voters and the Cumberland Town Council authorized a $700,000 bond for an 8,100-square-foot addition designed by Terrien Architects of Portland. Ground breaking occurred on October 10, 1986, and the new Cumberland Wing was dedicated on October 1, 1987. The children's room graduated from the basement of the original building into the new wing, along with the majority of the library's books and materials. The original building, renamed the Prince Room, was renovated into a community meeting space. The construction of the Cumberland Wing occurred during the period when Martha B. Pawle served as librarian.

YOUNG ADULT ROOM. The Prince Memorial Library Young Adult Challenge launched on January 18, 1995, when an anonymous Cumberland resident pledged $35,000, on the condition that an equal amount could be raised. The Town of Cumberland matched the $35,000, and private contributions amounted to an additional $45,745. The 728-square-foot Young Adult Room was dedicated on April 3, 1996, and has become a favored spot for the library's young people to hang out, read books, and play games. Prince Memorial Library had developed as former librarian Mildred Doane envisioned when she spoke on October 6, 1948, at the 25th anniversary of the library: "I hope that we shall have developed a group of readers who will grow up to be thinking men and women, leaders in their communities who will bring their children to this or other libraries to find, as they have, the magic of books."

Eight
SOCIAL ORGANIZATIONS

During the mid-to-late-19th century, Cumberland residents sought ways of cultivating special interests. No longer content only to meet and discuss matters at the general store or blacksmith's shop, residents began to form organizations in which they could pursue hobbies and shared passions. Some organizations were informal and spontaneous. In the 1850s and 1860s, after classes were dismissed for the day, several brick schoolhouses were transformed into gathering places for neighbors. Adults held singing and spelling schools. Skits dramatized stories from the novels by Sir Walter Scott and were performed in front of the long box stove. "Sings" were held in places such as the Buxton House, the Edmund Merrill House, and the Sweetser home. Singers were accompanied on the melodeon. Pennyroyals, hymns, and Irish tunes were popular. Children played parlor games such as Logomachy and Authors. Formal organizations included the Cumberland Brass Band, started in 1854 by Enos Blanchard, a sea captain, and continued until 1880. In 1889, a small group of white men formed the Red Men Sagwa Tribe No. 20. A national movement at the time, the Improved Order of Red Men purported to focus on temperance, patriotism, American history, and belief in a "Great Spirit, Creator and Preserver of the Universe," while appropriating or inventing rituals and regalia from Native American stereotypes. Its female auxiliary, the Daughters of Pocahontas, restricted membership to white women. In 1895, in response to several local men-only organizations like the Red Men and the Farmer's Club, a group of Cumberland women gathered to explore literature, the arts, history, and other avenues for learning. Officially founded as the We Neighbors Club in 1904 by Helen Davis, the club would continue to meet fortnightly for the next 100 years. In 1921, the West Cumberland Community Club, a social, literary, and charitable organization headed by Lizzie Copp, raised money to build a community hall, which officially opened in December 1922.

CUMBERLAND BRASS BAND. This c. 1875 photograph shows the Cumberland Brass Band in full regalia, complete with epaulets and hats with plumes. Instruments included tubas, euphoniums, trombones, French horns, trumpets, cornets, and a bass drum labeled "Cumberland Center Brass Band." The band was a Cumberland organization from 1854 until at least 1880.

DRAMATIC ENTERTAINMENT. Both the Auxillium Club and the Greely Institute Club periodically organized dramatic entertainment. This 1886 performance of *The Last Loaf* included well-known local residents such as George Blanchard, Frank Chase, J.B. Thomes, Ida S. Osgood, and Annie O. Buxton. Music often included Howard Buxton, known as the best tenor in town.

ORGANIZED SPORTS IN CUMBERLAND. In this photograph, the Cumberland Center baseball team poses in their team uniforms along with their manager. From left to right are (first row) Maurice Hayes, shortstop, and Ripley Burnell, first base; (second row) Whitman Dunn, field, and Lawrence Loring, field; (third row), Irwin Collins, manager; Carroll Wilson, third base; Ralph Burnell, field; Eli Burnell, pitcher; Everett Sweetser, second base; and Perry Burnell, catcher. Basketball also became popular in Cumberland in the early 1900s. The first recorded basketball game in Cumberland was played in 1904, in an outdoor field with baskets fastened to the top of poles. The new sport, introduced in 1891 by a Canadian teacher to keep students active indoors on rainy days, captured the attention of the Cumberland community quickly, and by 1911, arrangements were made to allow basketball games in Union Hall and the church vestry. Despite far from satisfactory conditions, people crowded into the limited space to watch games.

IMPROVED ORDER OF RED MEN. The Improved Order of Red Men was a community organization formed solely by and for white men, modeled on Boston revolutionaries, with rituals and regalia appropriated from stereotypes of Native American culture. By the late 19th century, the Red Men had attracted 519,942 members across 46 states. On April 27, 1914, Florence Merrill Blanchard, wife of then "sachem" Harvey Blanchard, and Bessie Powell Burnell, both members of the auxiliary group Daughters of Pocahontas, broke ground for the new Red Men's Hall next to the Congregational church. The new hall also became a community center with a polished dance floor and a large stage for amateur theatricals. In 1936, despite resistance, the town purchased the Red Men's Hall for $3,500. Elected in 1965, Bruce Jordan (below) became the new sachem of Sagwa Tribe No. 20.

WE NEIGHBORS CLUB, 1908. Motivated by curiosity and concern for one another, early We Neighbors members were eager to enrich their minds. They explored literary and artistic masterpieces such as Tennyson's *Idylls of the King* and Milton's *Paradise Lost*. The club also made plans for a field day every year, often to explore the surrounding towns, islands, and lakeshores. On June 23, 1908, they traveled 14 miles from Portland to Old Orchard on the electric railway for 20¢. From Old Orchard, they went to Camp Ellis, on a peninsula at the mouth of the Saco River, and enjoyed the basket lunch they had brought with them. One member recalled, "One of the great events of the day was souvenir pictures of our group taken at Newport Studio, Old Orchard." From left to right are (first row) Edith Whitney and Lizzie Tar; (second row) Abbie Thomes, Evelina Dunn, Evelyn Sweetser, and Mary Sweetser; (third row) Florence Sturdivant, Cora Adams, Laura Wyman, Elizabeth Buxton, Edith Sawyer, and May Doughty.

We Neighbors Club, 1913. On June 26, 1913, the We Neighbors Club held its annual field day on Peaks Island as guests of Mrs. F.N. Calderwood. Due to inclement weather, only seven members attended, leaving Portland on the 10:30 a.m. steamer. Bessie P. Burnell wrote, "[W]e were cordially welcomed by Mr. and Mrs. Calderwood. A short walk brought us to the cottage where we were greeted by Mrs. Huston, daughter of the hostess. Two open fires added much to our comfort as the day was chilly. . . . Our picnic dinner was eaten on the piazza—the hostess kindly supplying coffee and ice cream. After dinner we were entertained with solos by Schumann, Heink, Calve, and Melba, after which Mrs. Huston gave us several selections on the piano. We then had a group picture taken on the steps of the cottage." From left to right, the photograph includes (first row) Bessie Burnell, Mary Sweetser, Eveline Sweetser, and Evelina Dunn; (second row) Emma Buxton, Nellie Sweetser, Elizabeth Buxton, and Elizabeth Blanchard, (third row) the hosts Mr. and Mrs. Calderwood and their daughter Alice Huston.

WE NEIGHBORS CLUB, 1936. On August 5, 1936, We Neighbors held a field day picnic at Harriet Merrill's camp on Highland Lake, with some 19 members in attendance. The committee, composed of Bessie Burnell and Jennie Barter, "served a delicious picnic lunch. Bathing was enjoyed by some. We were very sorry some were kept away by sickness. A most enjoyable day was spent by those present."

WE NEIGHBORS CLUB, 1937. We Neighbors held its 1937 annual field day at Harriet Merrill's camp on the shore of Casco Bay in South Freeport on July 21. Sixteen members and five guests were present. "The weather was ideal and the setting perfect," Bessie Burnell wrote, "which gave all a delightful outing. A picnic lunch was enjoyed at noon."

ADDITIONAL ORGANIZATIONS. Other organizations included the Cumberland Historical Society, the Cumberland Garden Club, the Lions Club, the Nu-Cumbers Club in the 1960s, the Country Club, and a variety of youth and extracurricular organizations. The Garden Club, founded in 1956, studied horticulture and encouraged environmental projects. In the photograph above, members of the Garden Club show off flower-inspired hats at one of their events. Below, four members from the local Lions Club polish an automobile. Organized in 1961 with 25 charter members, the Lions Club engages the community in a variety of charitable events, including providing eye-care services for those in need and sponsoring scholarships for Greely students.

Nine
HOUSES

Houses are often the most durable and intimate artifacts that survive from the day-to-day lives of past generations. At the same time, they illustrate the way a place or structure is slowly transformed by necessity, fashion, or time. A single house might stay in one family for a century or more, but additions, alterations, and renovations reflect their eras so much that, in the end, what remains is a palimpsest of the generations who came before. Cumberland, like many small New England towns, witnessed a range of architectural styles that remain evident in the houses and barns still standing today. Eighteenth-century houses, now largely altered, give a good idea of what many of the first houses may have looked like: functional, simple, and lacking the embellishments of houses from later, more comfortable eras. A center chimney, which evenly dispersed heat throughout the house, is common throughout Cumberland. Small-paned windows, shutters, and narrow doorways were also typical for the time. In the early 19th century, during the Federal period, houses became more elaborate, including details like fan doorways, locally made brick, and granite lintel over the windows. In the mid-19th century, Greek Revival architecture flourished, with one-and-a-half-story houses, wings, and ells, and by the 1860s, the Victorian period popularized overhanging eaves, stove chimneys, bay windows, double doors with glass insets, porches, and ornate details. Several sites in Cumberland that began as locations for private homes now host important historical or municipal buildings, such as Prince Memorial Library, which stands where both Rev. Rufus Anderson's and Benjamin Sweetser's families once lived. Likewise, buildings that were once public fixtures in the community, such as the Leighton Tavern and the Winn Road schoolhouse, are now given over to private space.

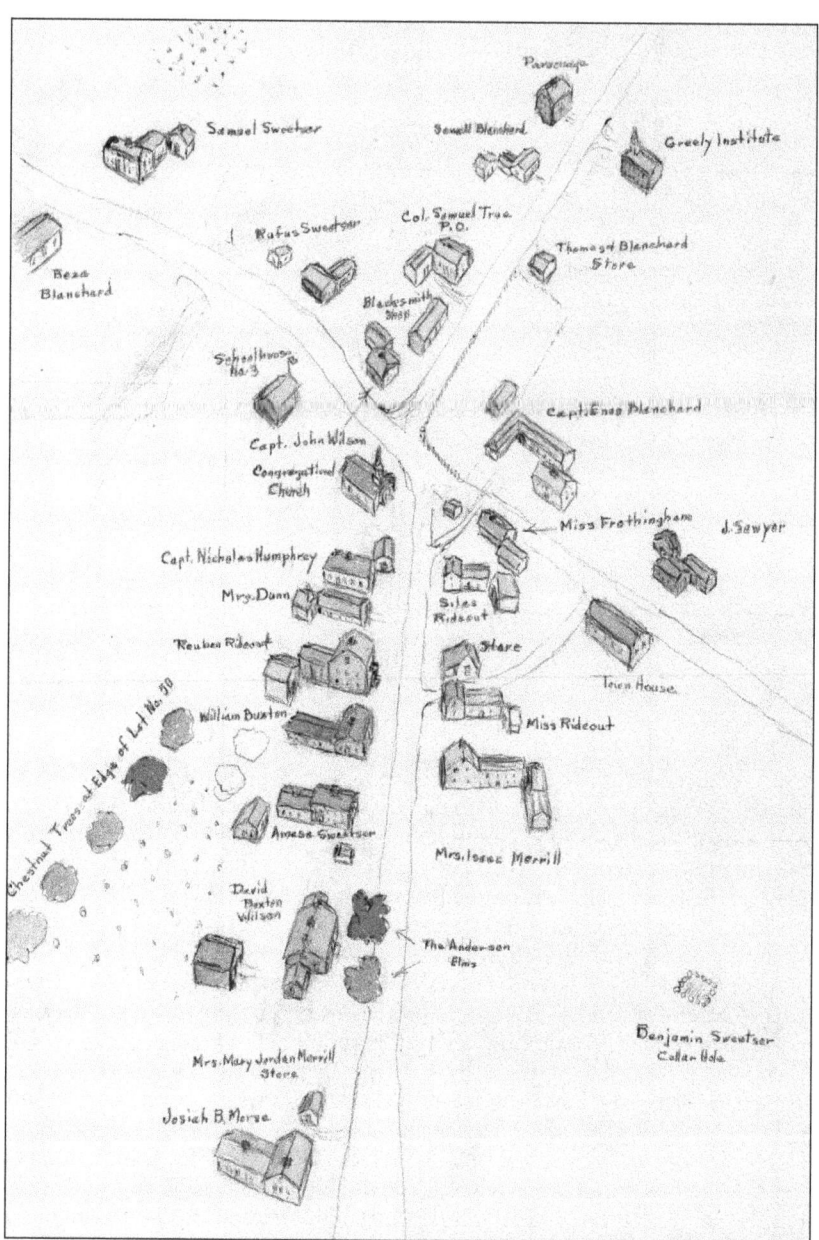

INSET OF HOPE DILLAWAY MAP. Hope Dillaway (1910–2004) created her index *Locating the Old Houses of Cumberland, Maine* by compiling data from the 1857 Map of Cumberland County and the 1871 Atlas of Cumberland County. The 1857 map is from surveys produced by J. Chace Jr. of Philadelphia and includes names of residents, inset maps of villages and towns, population statistics, table of distances, and local businesses for all the towns in Cumberland County. The 1871 Atlas of Cumberland County was made from actual surveys by and under the direction of F.W. Beers, with assistance from George P. Sanford and others, and was published by F.W. Beers & Co. of New York. The Dillaway map, based on the 1857 and 1871 maps, serves as an index, with each building in the town numbered and referencing a homeowner, business, or building type. The Dillaway map is 105 by 105 centimeters and includes watercolor sketches of some of Cumberland's oldest buildings along the intersection of Main Street and Blanchard and Tuttle Roads.

AMASA SMITH HOUSE. Rev. Amasa Smith was widely regarded as an unusual choice for the pastor of the Congregational Church in Cumberland in 1806. Prior to becoming a minister, Smith had served as a minuteman in the American Revolution and ran a tavern in his hometown of Belcherville, Massachusetts. With 10 children, many of whom could not yet support themselves, he and his wife, Sophia, required a good-sized home. In 1820, following the Halfway Covenant, which he believed reflected a weakening of moral ideals, Smith asked to be dismissed from the church. Instead, he traveled to small villages without ministers to preach until, at 78, he became too tired to travel. He died in 1849 at the age of 91. His son Col. Joseph Smith was the master-builder behind four Cumberland churches, including Cumberland Congregational.

OCTOBER FARM. October Farm on Tuttle Road was the home of James Tuttle, who purchased the hundred-acre lot No. 46 in 1731. The house is believed to have been built in 1763 and was later owned by Asa and Hannah Mitchell Chase, followed by William and Hannah Merrill Reed. October Farm was never a specialty operation, but a subsistence farm, and featured a traditional big house, little house, back house, and barn configuration.

FRANK MERRILL HOUSE. In 1807, Josiah B. Morse married Abigail Sweetser and bought 25 acres near the home of her brother Benjamin Sweetser. Morse worked as a cobbler in a little building on the northern side of the property, which the women of the family would later convert into a dressmaking shop. Morse's daughter Mary Jordan Sweetser, a talented seamstress, and her husband, Rufus Merrill, inherited the house.

EPHRAIM STURDIVANT HOUSE. The house at 114 Foreside Road was built by Capt. Ephraim Sturdivant in 1810. The interior woodwork was lavish for the time, with flourishes like a ribbon carving around the fireplace, chair rail, and cornice. On the hill behind the house stood 12 tall pines recognized by ships mooring in Portland Harbor as the Twelve Apostles; the last of these pines fell in 1935.

SAMUEL SWEETSER HOUSE. In 1812, Deacon Jeremiah Blanchard built the house at 15 Blanchard Road for Mary Ann Pittee, a widow. In 1849, her son-in-law Samuel R. Sweetser purchased property from the Blanchard estate for $190 and transformed it into the thriving Sweetser orchards. In this 1875 photograph, Samuel and Frederick Sweetser sit in front of the house with an unidentified man; apple trees can be seen to the left of the house.

Beza Blanchard House and Reuben Blanchard House. Capt. Beza Blanchard Sr., the sea captain who started Spring Brook Farm in 1820 with 110 acres of farmland, lived in the house below with his wife, Prudence, and their 12 children. Members of the Blanchard family pictured are, from left to right, Dorcas Prince Blanchard, Mildred M. Blanchard, David Loring Blanchard, Ethel Cameron Blanchard, and Mary Tewksbury Blanchard. Beza's son Capt. Reuben Blanchard assumed ownership of Spring Brook in 1825 and raised his family in the house above. In this 1880 photograph, Reuben and his wife, Christiana, are seated, while son Frank and his wife, Elizabeth, are standing behind them. Grandsons Harry (left) and Fred are standing on either side.

BENJAMIN SWEETSER HOUSE. Around 1835, Benjamin Sweetser, deciding that he would prefer to live nearer the well-established main road, bought the old Parson Anderson place, and built where the former house had been what was then a new idea: a duplex house with an efficient apartment on each side. He and his wife, Dolly, took up residence on the south side, while his newlywed son Rufus lived with his wife on the northern side. In 1848, Rufus had moved to support his wife's family, so his young sister Elizabeth and her new husband, Capt. David Wilson, moved into his apartment. Thirty years later, the northern side passed to their son William's family, and later their daughter Elizabeth, before it was rented out to various tenants. In 1906, the house burned, and Maude Merrill, Capt. Wilson's niece, acquired the land. She eventually donated it as the site of Prince Memorial Library.

SILAS RIDEOUT HOUSE. This house, built around 1820, was first the home of an elderly Quaker. Later, it was used as a schoolhouse where Jane Wilson taught. In 1827, the first actual schoolhouse was built opposite the church, and Silas Rideout bought this house, set up his carriage business next door, and lived here for the rest of his life.

JENNIE SOULE DUNN HOUSE. Between Reuben Rideout's place and Nathaniel Humphrey's store, sometime in the 1870s, this house was built for the widow of Cyrus Dunn and her son James. They had come from North Yarmouth, and James Dunn planned to open a business like his father's general store. In time, he became the proprietor of the store across the street.

OLIVE HALL HOUSE. After Dr. Frank Hall's death in 1872, his widow, Olive M. Hall, moved across the street with her daughter to a newly placed house just north of the Silas Rideout house, seen here on the left. Previously, it was the old store building and millinery shop that had stood just above on Tuttle Road. It was moved and refurbished as a dwelling, serving first Olive Hall and other tenants down the years.

ARNO CHASE HOUSE. In the mid-1890s, Arno Chase built a new house at Cumberland Center just north of Olive Hall's house, in the same place where her house had stood as a shop before it was moved. Behind it, he built the extensive greenhouse where for over 40 years he carried on an active florist business.

COPP HOMESTEAD, C. 1890. John Franklin Copp, who came from the Liberty, Maine, area, married Mary Etta Black in 1883, and they lived in this house for several years. Mary Etta was the daughter of Joab Black Jr. and Sara Jane Libby. Mary Etta died in 1901, and around 1916, John Copp and his daughter Elizabeth relocated this building to the northern edge of the property and built a new home in its place. The Copp homestead fell down in the mid-1900s.

WILLIAM WILSON HOUSE. In 1890, William Wilson began to build a home for his wife and four daughters on the lot between his grandfather Benjamin Sweetser's house and that of Amasa Sweetser. Having worked as a carpenter in California, Wilson incorporated new architectural ideas into the plans of his dream home. The house was fully realized by 1900, just in time for his fifth daughter to be born in their new home.

HANSON FAMILY HOMESTEAD, C. 1902. This photograph of the Hanson family in front of their home was taken around 1902. The barn on the left was built in 1893; the main house on the right, which remains standing today, was built in 1896 or 1897. A shed and kitchen connect both structures in the background. From left to right in the yard stand brothers Grover (age nine), Hans (eighteen), Henry (fourteen), family friend Olga Nelson (one), and father, Hans Henrik, with mother Maren (Jensen) on the porch. The Hanson family came to Maine from Denmark, where Hans Henrik, Maren, and the two older sons were born. Prior to their arrival in Maine, Hans Henrik Hanson help settle New Denmark in Canada with his brother Anders Laurits Hanson. After Hans Henrik died in 1921, Maren continued the farm alone, making cheese and raising vegetables, chickens, and eggs. In 1945, Hans Hanson and his wife, Tina, moved into the house and installed running water and a modern bathroom. (Courtesy of Phil Stanhope.)

DAVID SPEAR HOUSE AND ROUTE 88. The image on this postcard was taken in the 1920s and shows Foreside Road at the junction of King's Highway and Town Landing Road. The house, once the home of both David Spear Sr., and David Spear Jr., has the Portland & Yarmouth Electric Railway tracks in front of it. At the base of the utility pole on the right is the B136 mile marker for the King's Highway, designating that Boston is 136 miles away. Spear's shipyard, at the end of Town Landing Road, was one of many shipyards on Casco Bay. A family business owned and operated by David Spear Sr., then David Spear Jr., the shipyard built over 50 vessels in the 1800s, including six schooners, four ships, two barks, and seventeen brigs. Steam power, steel ships, and the rising cost of wood brought an end to the shipbuilding era, and David Spear Jr.'s last three ships lost him over $20,000. He was forced to give up the shipyard and other properties to settle his debts and started over as a laborer, earning less than a dollar a day.

Ten

People

The study of a single life often reveals much about the time in which it was lived. Sweeping generational changes like war, revolution, prejudice, and innovation reverberate throughout history, influencing personal lifestyles and choices. What is represented in this chapter is only a sliver of the past residents of Cumberland, those with the means and opportunity to have their portraits made, and those whose photographs have survived long enough to be recorded in this book. Due to the bias of history, the majority of those pictured here are men; all those in this chapter are white. Nor does this book contain much information on the indigenous people who were pushed from their territory by white settlers. Despite the violence on which the settlement that would become Cumberland was founded, for the larger part of history, its community has pursued peaceful lives as farmers, schoolteachers, sea captains, shipbuilders, shopkeepers, and librarians. Family names that are prolific and recurring in Cumberland history include the Blacks; the Blanchards, responsible for both the Broadmoor and Spring Brook farms, as well as several sea captains; the Chases, involved in both the fire department and the carnation industry; the Merrills; the Princes, for whom Prince Tavern and Prince Memorial Library were named; the Sturdivants; and the Sweetsers, of Sweetser's Apple Barrel and Orchard. No less significant are the families and individuals who immigrated to Cumberland from elsewhere and the Cumberland natives who moved away when they were young and, for whatever reason, did not return. What began in 1821 as a town of 1,386 souls has, over the past two centuries, grown to include over 7,200 individuals spread across over 2,600 households.

EPHRAIM STURDIVANT. Ephraim Sturdivant (1772–1868) went to sea at age 12 and gained command of a vessel before he was 21. Sturdivant participated in the War of 1812 after he received permission to operate the *Reaper* and the *Ilsley* as privateers. He married three times between 1809 and 1843 and fathered 21 children. He is credited with giving the town its name and served in the Maine legislature and as town selectman and treasurer for many years.

JOSEPH BLANCHARD. Joseph Blanchard (1803–1884) left home at the age of 14 aboard the schooner *Telegraph*. He captained several brigs and made at least four ocean crossings before he built a ship of his own. He sailed the *Cornelia* between the United States and Europe for the next eight years. Over the course of his career, he made 84 voyages to the West Indies and another 30 to Europe.

CONGREGATIONAL CHURCH 100TH ANNIVERSARY. The Congregational Church's elders helped celebrate the church's 100th anniversary on September 21, 1893. From left to right are (first row, seated) Margaret Wilson, Mrs. Benjamin Sweetser, Joanne Blanchard, Sarah Buxton, Mrs. Blake, Harriet Blanchard, and Jane Merrill; (second row, standing) Samuel Sweetser, Capt. Beza Blanchard, John Blanchard, Josiah Haskell, and Silas Rideout.

CONGREGATIONAL CHURCH 150TH ANNIVERSARY. At the church's 150th anniversary in 1943, the older members of the congregation posed for a photograph. From left to right are (first row) Annie F. Sturdivant, Laura Herrick Wyman, Alice Sawyer Doughty, Emily Norton Wilson, Evaline Merrill Sweetser, and Elizabeth Sweetser Greely; (second row) Fred Adams, Arno S. Chase, Horatio H. Herrick, Edward B. Osgood, Samuel S.J. Porter, J. Edward Warren, and Samuel Ross.

SCOTT LEIGHTON. Scott Leighton (1847–1898) was born in West Cumberland and grew up in Gray, where he began working with horses at a young age. By 17, Leighton saved enough money trading horses to move to Portland to attempt a career as an artist. Finding no luck in Maine, he moved to Boston and opened a studio sometime before 1880. Leighton painted many prominent horses, as well as barnyard and landscape scenes. He was an artist in the Currier and Ives workshop.

FRANK MERRILL. The Cumberland Center post office was at many locations in town between 1829 and 1947, when it moved to Farwell Avenue. For many years, it was in the Blanchard Brothers general store. When the store burned, the post office was temporarily relocated but returned to 277 Main Street when J.L. Dunn opened his general store. In this c. 1900 photograph, Frank Merrill (1854–1963) sits in the post office in J.L. Dunn's store.

FRANK BLANCHARD, 1918 ARMISTICE CELEBRATION. Francis "Frank" W. Blanchard (1838–1926) served in the Union Navy during the Civil War as the paymaster on the steamer *Yankee*. His father, Reuben Blanchard (1794–1887), was a ship captain who inherited Spring Brook Farm in 1825. When Frank returned from war, he took over the farm and married Elizabeth H. Sweetser, with whom he had two sons, Harry and Fred. In the 1920s, Spring Brook made and sold about 100 pounds of butter annually; when the market dropped in 1931, Spring Brook switched to wholesale milk. The farm passed through several generations of Blanchard men until 1971, when Katherine Blanchard Fowler and her husband, Greg, partnered with Stanley Blanchard, Katherine's father. Today, Spring Brook still operates and focuses on ecologically responsible farming practices. Blanchard, at left in the back seat, participates in a 1918 Armistice celebration.

FLOYD AND ADA NORTON. Floyd Wilson Norton (1891–1988) was born to Charles and Lizzie Norton in Cumberland on April 14, 1891. At age 20, he traveled the country and worked as a telegraph operator in California, New Mexico, and Wyoming. He was a Western Union manager in Lewiston, Bridgton, and Indiana; worked for seven different railroads and several newspapers; and operated a ground telegraph unit during World War II. He taught school in Maine, Colorado, Arizona, and Idaho, and was an instructor during a 10-year stint in the Air Force. Throughout his life, he lived and worked in 46 states and is credited with building some of the first snowmobiles in the country. In 1942, he married teacher Ada Odessa Myers, and in 1964, the couple retired to Yarmouth. Floyd died on May 13, 1988, at the age of 97; Ada died on June 7, 1997, at the age of 103. Floyd was the author of *Norton's Hand-Hewn History of Maine and Its Representative Town of Cumberland* and an accomplished photographer. In this photograph, he and Ada stand together in front of their 1950 Zündapp motorcycle.

ARNO CHASE. Arno Chase (1862–1954), along with his brother Frank, began a greenhouse business selling plants from a painted wagon. By the early 1900s, each had their own commercial greenhouses, accounting for two of four in the town. Arno Chase's greenhouse burned in March 1933, but he was able to rebuild and recover his business.

EDWARD B. OSGOOD. Edward B. "Deacon" Osgood (1860–1944) was one of the six first graduates from Greely Institute in June 1880. He opened a general store in the 1880s, and by 1900 listed his business as a merchant of meats and provisions. In addition to smoked meats sold from his small shop, Osgood ran a profitable packing plant. His grandson Fred took over when Osgood died in 1944.

Samuel S.J. Porter. In addition to serving as the deacon of the Congregational church, Samuel S.J. Porter (1866–1944) was one of Cumberland's first rural postmen, along with his brother Ralph, and served as a mail carrier for 28 years. He was involved in many local social organizations, including the Red Men. This photograph from 1904 captures Porter delivering mail to a young Jeannette Sturdivant on Tuttle Road.

Lizzie M. Copp. Lizzie M. Copp (1884–1976) was a Cumberland teacher and the first president of the West Cumberland Community Club, a social, literary, and charitable organization. Although it initially held potlucks in private homes, the club raised enough money to build a community club in West Cumberland through suppers, entertainment, and a lawn party where members sold aprons, ice cream, and home-cooked food. The hall opened on September 16, 1922.

KENNETH CHASE. Kenneth W. Chase (1902–1979) was Cumberland's fire chief from 1936 to 1942. In a 1976 interview, he recalled how residents met in 1929 and formed a volunteer fire department. Chase also drove the town's first school bus, a 1929 Ford Model A with a 40-pupil capacity. He covered the whole town and all of the one-room schools, primarily driving on dirt roads.

HERB FOSTER SR. In 1949, after a plea by selectmen to expand the select board and hire a clerk, Herbert S. Foster Sr. (1901–1973) was hired to the newly created position and elected town clerk and town treasurer. Foster served in all three positions until 1973, when the new council-manager form of government was instituted in Cumberland.

GREELY INSTITUTE CLASS OF 1946. The Greely Institute class of 1946 poses for a photograph. From left to right are (kneeling) Russell Barter, Willis "Bill" Raymond Thurston, and Dick Anderson; (standing) Christine Phoebe Gregor, Frances Evelyn Trufant, Jean Lorraine Burnell, Jean Laurel Fisk, Gloria Estelle Verrill, Patricia Holbrook, Joan Middlesworth, Evelyn Hope Frye, and Myrtie Allen.

MABEL I. WILSON. Mabel Wilson (1904–1998) was born in Dubuque, Iowa, and earned a bachelor's degree from the University of Dubuque. While studying at Yale Medical School, she met Melville Morrison Wilson. They married in 1926 and moved to Mel's family home in Cumberland. Mabel taught school in Cumberland and served on the town's school and budget committees before retiring at age 68. Mabel I. Wilson School is named in her honor.

BIBLIOGRAPHY

Bennett, Thomas C. *"Changes in Character of Response": Population Decline in Cumberland, Maine, 1860–1920.* Cumberland, ME: Prince Memorial Library, 2019. https://digitalmaine.com/cumberland_books/78.

Clayton, W. Woodford. *History of Cumberland County, Maine: With Illustrations and Biographical Sketches of Its Prominent Men and Pioneers.* Philadelphia, PA: Everts & Peck, 1880.

Corliss, Augustus Whittemore. *Old times of North Yarmouth, Maine: A Facsimile of the Thirty-two Quarterly Magazines Edited and Published by Augustus W. Corliss as Well as the Single Issue of The Wescustogo Chronicle, 1877–1885.* Somersworth, NH: New Hampshire Publishing, 1977.

Dillaway, Hope and Thomas C. Bennett. *Locating the Old Houses of Cumberland Maine.* Cumberland, ME: Prince Memorial Library, 2014. https://digitalmaine.com/cumberland_books/2.

Hauk, Zarah William. *The Stone Sloops of Chebeague and the Men Who Sailed Them; also Some Chebeague Miscellany.* Boston, MA: Alden-Hauk, 1953.

Joy, Wendy L. *Wildwood: the Story of a Neighborhood.* Cumberland, ME: Wildwood Association, 2000.

Merrill, Sally A. *Cumberland, Maine: Carnation Capital of the Country?* Cumberland, ME: Prince Memorial Library, 2016. https://digitalmaine.com/ cumberland_books /56.

———. *Records of We Neighbors Club Cumberland, Maine 1895–1995.* Cumberland, ME: Prince Memorial Library, 2016. https://digitalmaine.com/ cumberland_books /51.

Mitchell, H.E, R.C. Russell, and W. R Strout. *The Cumberland and No. Yarmouth Register.* Brunswick, ME: The H.E. Mitchell Pub. Co., 1904. https://lccn.loc.gov/12019875.

Norton, Floyd. *Norton's Hand-Hewn History of Maine and Its Representative Town of Cumberland.* Cumberland, ME: Prince Memorial Library, 2017. https://digitalmaine.com/cumberland_books/61/

Rowe, William Hutchinson. *Ancient North Yarmouth and Yarmouth, Maine, 1636–1936.* Yarmouth, ME: New England History Press, 1937.

Sweetser, Mary E. *History of the Town of Cumberland, Maine.* Yarmouth, ME: A.F. Tilton, 1921. https://digitalmaine.com/cumberland_books/9.

Sweetser, Phyllis Sturdivant. *Cumberland, Maine in Four Centuries.* Cumberland, ME: Town of Cumberland, 1976.

Town of Cumberland Annual Reports. digitalmaine.com/cumberland_annual_reports.

Visit us at
arcadiapublishing.com